James Bonner

A New Plan for Speedily Increasing the Number of Beehives in Scotland

James Bonner

A New Plan for Speedily Increasing the Number of Beehives in Scotland

ISBN/EAN: 9783337327644

Printed in Europe, USA, Canada, Australia, Japan

Cover: Foto ©Suzi / pixelio.de

More available books at **www.hansebooks.com**

A

NEW PLAN

FOR

SPEEDILY INCREASING

THE

NUMBER OF BEE-HIVES

IN

SCOTLAND;

AND WHICH MAY BE EXTENDED, WITH EQUAL SUCCESS,

TO

ENGLAND, IRELAND, AMERICA,

OR

TO ANY OTHER PART OF THE WORLD CAPABLE OF PRODUCING FLOWERS.

By JAMES BONNER, BEE-MASTER,

AUTHOR OF PRACTICAL WARPING MADE EASY, &c.

Though small's the Insect, great will be the Gain ;
If heavenly Powers permit, and Phoebus not disdain.

VIRG.

EDINBURGH:

PRINTED BY J. MOIR, PATERSON'S COURT:
SOLD BY W. CREECH, BELL & BRADFUTE, P. HILL, MUDIE & SON,
AND BY THE AUTHOR, AT MR GRANT'S, LEITH WYND,
EDINBURGH :—AND BY T. KAY, NO. 332.
STRAND, LONDON.

1795.

Price 4s. 6d.

TO THE

MOST NOBLE,

THE PRESIDENT,

AND THE OTHER

RIGHT HONOURABLE

AND HONOURABLE MEMBERS

OF THE

HIGHLAND SOCIETY OF SCOTLAND.

———

MY LORDS AND GENTLEMEN,

THE generous and diftinguifhed mark of
refpect already beftowed upon me, for my
fmall exertions in the fervice of the Public,
while it commanded my gratitude, at the fame
time emboldened me to folicit your Patronage
to the following fheets, wrote upon the important fubject which firft introduced me to your
notice. Your ready and unanimous acqui-
efcence, in granting me this additional honour,
with the particular favours I have received
from many of you, adds exceedingly to the

obligations

(ii)

obligations formerly beftowed, and calls for frefh ebullitions of my utmoft gratitude to you, both as a Society and as Individuals.

THAT your laudable endeavours, for promoting the good of your Country, in every refpect, may be crowned with the greateft fuccefs, and that both the prefent and future generations may be extenfively benefited by your public-fpirited and patriotic exertions, is the earneft wifh of,

MY LORDS AND GENTLEMEN,

Your moft obedient,

Moft obliged, and

Moft humble Servant,

JAMES BONNER.

EDINBURGH,
JULY 18. 1795.

PREFACE.

Biographers and Philosophers are equally puzzled to account for the great diverfity of talents among mankind, and the peculiar bent of genius to be found in each individual. While fome pretend to account for thefe peculiarities, from the accidental circumftances in which individuals happen to be placed, others, with at leaft equal probability, attribute them to peculiar inclinations, implanted by Nature, or rather the Author of Nature in the human mind. Perhaps both caufes muft co-operate to produce that degree of enthufiaftic fondnefs for particular purfuits, which, in all ages, has diftinguifhed fome individuals in every branch of fcience, or of art, and which is fo humoroufly entitled by the facetious Sterne, a man's Hobby Horse. *

The author of this work has been, almoft from his infancy, an admirer of bees, and the

a   fruit

* Triftram Shandy, vol. 1.

fruit of their labours. When a fchool-boy, he read with peculiar pleafure, the defcription given of CANAAN, as a land flowing with milk and HONEY.

Being appointed by his father,* when a boy, to watch his bees in fwarming time, his fondnefs for thefe wonderful infects daily increafed; and he could not help thinking himfelf in a kind of paradifaical ftate, when employed in this delightful office in his father's garden, and running

---

* The author's father, JAMES BONNER, was, like himfelf, fond of rearing bees, and often had a dozen of hives at a time in his garden. He lived above 50 years in the married ftate, and had twelve children, of whom the author is the youngeft alive. He frequently boafted, that, in good feafons, he made as much money by his bees, as nearly purchafed oat-meal fufficient to ferve his numerous family for the whole year. He purchafed a large quarto Bible with the wax produced in one year from his hives, which ferved as a family book ever after; and his houfe was always well fupplied with honey, and a kind of weak mead, which ferved for drink at all feafons of the year. As he lived regularly and temperately, he preferved a great degree of health and vigour to the laft; and was employed in his ordinary bufinefs of weaving, till within a few days of his death; which happened in the 86th year of his age, when he left four fons and a daughter, to regret his lofs. He had always an uncommonly retentive memory; for, upon the fmalleft hint, he could repeat almoft any paffage in fcripture verbatim. He ufed often to entertain his family with a narrative of his treatment of his bees, and of the profit, as well as pleafure, which he had in keeping them.

running among the blooming bufhes, and variegated flowers, to look after the young fwarms. When very young, he purchafed three hives, which he gradually increafed to a pretty large ftock, and has ever fince taken great pleafure, over and above every view of emolument, to ftudy the nature of thefe valuable infects, and to inveftigate the caufes of their thriving and unprofperous ftates; their health and difeafes; the beft means of preferving the individuals, and of propagating and multiplying their induftrious race, with their management in every refpect. For this purpofe, he has perufed with avidity every book in the Englifh language, on the fubject, that he could get accefs to; and has fpared neither time, trouble, nor expence, (having beftowed much indeed of both, beyond what he could well afford,) in trying numerous experiments upon them.*

a 2　　　　　But

* So great was the author's curiofity, and enthufiaftic attachment to the ftudy of the nature and properties of thefe curious infects, that, above twenty years ago, he went from Berwickfhire to London, on purpofe to converfe with Mr WILDMAN on the fubject; but that gentleman happening to be in France at the time, he contented himfelf with purchafing every book he could find on the management of bees, and has ever fince made it

his

But, however valuable and useful many of the treatises already publifhed on this fubject have been, he is confident, from the repeated obfervations and experiments he has made, that moft of them are not only defective, but even erroneous in many particulars ; and that the culture of bees in Britain ‡, has never yet arrived at any thing near that degree of perfection, to which it might be brought, if the fyftem which he has formed, and now fubmits to the public, were generally underftood and properly practifed. If we only confider the almoft infinite number of mellifluous flowers, which perfume the air in the honey feafon ; and. in particular, the white clover, which fo generally and profitably now overfpreads fo large a part of our lands in grafs ; the various rious

his chief pleafure, as well as bufinefs, to ftudy every poffible improvement refpecting that wonderful race. During the honey feafon, he has often been fo intent upon this ftudy, that he hardly allowed himfelf fleep for whole weeks together.

‡ Although the author, in making out his calculations relative to the increafe of Bee hives, was under the neceffity of confining himfelf to fome one particular country, and naturally made choice of his native land, his plan will, nevertheless, he is confident, apply with equal propriety to ENGLAND, IRELAND, AMERICA, or indeed any other part of the known world, capable of producing proper food for thefe infects.

rious fpecies of muftard, and plants of a fimilar kind, found ftill in our corn fields, together with the vaft abundance of heath, that
grows fpontaneoufly on our extenfive moors and
hills, we may juftly fay, how large and numerous are our pafture grounds, but how very
few are our flocks to feed on them!

A judicious author juftly obferves, that the
culture of bees is a branch of rural œconomy,
the more valuable, that it is within the reach
of the pooreft cottager, and requires neither
plowing, manure, cattle, nor rich meadows.
All that is wanted, is a fmall degree of attendance, which may be given by the meaneft, as
it is requifite only for a fhort time; and therefore the plentiful harveft of honey and wax
that is produced, may be confidered as fo many RICH CROPS REAPED WITHOUT SOWING.

As nothing is fo hurtful to bees as bad weather, fo nothing can be fo little counteracted;
although even the bad effects of it may, in
fome meafure, be prevented; for, we can preferve our bees in cold and fnowy winters, by
confining them; and, in a late fpring, or rainy
fummer, we can preferve them from famine, by
feeding them properly. But, even in the moft
unfavourable weather, I never defpond; for

I

I have obferved, that in the very worſt ſeaſons, and notwithſtanding the ſmall number
of hives; that there are in Scotland, a tolerable quantity of honey is always produced :
And therefore, had there been 20 times more
hives in the kingdom, and a few flowers artificially raiſed, with proper attention, there
would have been, even in theſe very bad ſeaſons, juſt 20 times as much honey and wax
collected as there was : and in good ſeaſons,
ſuch as laſt year, (1794) when there was a
great deal of honey produced, even from our
ſmall ſtock of hives, what an immenſe quantity would have been collected, had there been
forty or fifty times more ſtock hives in ſpring !

Impreſſed with theſe ideas, and anxious to
do all in his power to promote an object ſo beneficial to the country at large, as well as to
individuals, the author firſt ventured to lay
his ſentiments before the public in 1789, by
publiſhing a Treatiſe on the Management of
Bees, which, he was happy to find, attracted
the notice, and procured him the patronage, of
many reſpectable and public-ſpirited gentlemen. Encouraged by theſe flattering marks
of approbation, he had thoughts of publiſhing a ſecond edition ; but as, in the conti-

nued

PREFACE.

nued profecution of this his favourite ftudy, he has made a number of very important dif- coveries relative to thefe ufeful infects, he thought it better to prefent thefe new ideas, along with the fubftance of his former work, compreffed into as fmall bounds as poffible, in a new form, and under a new title, than mere- ly to reprint the old work with additions. And the chief object of the prefent perform- ance being to excite the attention of the pub- lic in general, but efpecially of gentlemen in opulent circumftances, to the rearing of bees, by fhowing them the PRACTICABILITY of in- creafing the number of bee-hives in this coun- try at leaft TWENTY-FOLD, if not to FIFTY times the number there are at prefent, he thought it proper to entitle the whole mafs of old and new matter, " A New Plan for fpeedi- " ly increafing the number of Bee-Hives in " Scotland, &c."

Nor is it to his literary labours alone, that he has been indebted for the liberal encou- ragement he has met with. In his *commercial* concerns, as a dealer in honey, he has been ho- noured with the patronage and employment of a number of the nobility and gentry in Edinburgh, Newcaftle, and many other places ;

for

for which he embraces this opportunity of returning them his beſt thanks. And here he cannot help mentioning a circumſtance which he eſteems peculiarly fortunate, as it introduced him to the employment and patronage of that reſpectable patriot, the PRESIDENT OF THE BOARD OF AGRICULTURE; whoſe exerons for the improvement of his country, and general benefit of ſociety, far exceed his praiſe. One morning in autumn laſt (1794) as the author was carrying a few very fine honey combs, to a gentleman in the New Town, he was met by Sir John Sinclair, whom previouſly he did not know, * and was deſired to bring to him ſome of his fine honey next morning. This he accordingly did, and a converſation having enſued, reſpecting the time he had ſpent in the culture of bees, the number of hives he kept, &c. &c. he was deſired by the public-ſpirited Baronet to draw up a plan for the rearing of bees in a more extenſive manner: and the author having executed this taſk to the beſt of

his

---

* About a year before this, ſeveral gentlemen had deſired the author to wait upon Sir JOHN SINCLAIR, and lay before him a plan for the rearing of bees; but diffidence always prevented him, and probably ever would, if Providence had not brought about the interview in ſome ſuch manner as the above-mentioned.

his abilities, Sir John Sinclair was kind enough to lay it before the Highland Society, who were so good as to honour him with one of their highest premiums, for his unremitting and successful attention, during a period of no less than 26 years, in acquiring a knowledge of the operations of bees ; and for the various discoveries made by him, tending to multiply the number of hives, and quantity of honey and wax in this kingdom, contained in his communications to the society, and now laid before the public, in this treatise.

This encouragement led the author to hope, that his plan might turn out to be generally a-dopted, if once universally known. He there-fore distributed subscription papers, in order to try the minds of the public in general ; and in doing this, his success far exceeded his most sanguine expectations ; for he scarcely met with one in an hundred, who did not ap-prove of his plan ; as will appear from the respectable list of subscriptions prefixed to this work, and which might have been rendered greatly more numerous, if the author's time and other avocations had permitted him to circulate his proposals more generally.

The author, therefore, without farther apology, now fubmits his plan to the attention of the public; and he has not a doubt, but that, if the directions therein given are ftrictly adhered to, and perfevered in by gentlemen of property, and the public in general, in a few years Scotland will not only fave much money now fent abroad for honey and wax, but will even be able to render them articles of export.

He needs only add, that, in the following treatife, he has not, as too many authors in all branches of fcience are apt to do, ftrained any arguments to fupport a favourite hypothefis: But, on the contrary, his whole theory and practice being founded on experience and facts, he flatters himfelf, that he has delivered his fentiments throughout the work, in a manner fo plain and intelligible, that the moft unlettered reader will not miftake his meaning.

Names

NAMES OF THE SUBSCRIBERS.

A

Jacob Atkinfon, Efq; Newcaftle

Reverend Mr Allifon, Newburn

Mr James Arbuthnot, jun. Peterhead,

Meffrs Allan and Weft, bookfellers, No. 15, Paternofter-row, London, 12 copies

Mr Alexander Aitchifon, ftudent of phyfic, Edinburgh

B

Colonel Baillie, of Rofehall, 2 copies

Reverend Doctor George Baird, principal of the Univerfity of Edinburgh

John Balfour, Efq; of Balbirnie

A. Barclay, Efq; W. S. Edinburgh

John Bell, Efq; of Gallow-hill 2 copies

Benjamin Bell, Efq; furgeon, Edinburgh

Andrew Bell, Efq; engraver, Edinburgh

William Beveridge, Efq; W. S. Edin.

David Black, Efq; Dunfermline

John Bogue, Efq; of Halydown

William Bogue, Efq; of Greenburn

Thomfon Bonnar, Efq; Edinburgh

Alexander Bofwell, Efq; of Auchenleck

George Brown, Efq; one of the Commiffioners of Excife, Edinburgh

Thomas Bruce, Efq; of Arnot, 2 copies

Thomas Bruce, Efq; of Kennet

Edward Bruce, Efq; W. S. Edinburgh

Arthur Bruce, Efq; Secretary to the Natural Hiftory Society, Edinburgh

John Buchan, Efq; W. S. Edinburgh

Mr John Buchan, accountant, Edinburgh

Hector M'Donald Buchanan, Efq; W. S. Edinburgh

John Butter, Efq; of Benbecula

Captain Abraham Bunbury

Reverend Mr George Bowe, Shilbottle

Reverend Mr John Brodie, Kinloch

Reverend Mr Laurence Butler, Lethendy

Meffrs Bell and Bradfute, bookfellers, Edinburgh, 6 copies

Meffrs Beilby and Bewick, Newcaftle

Mrs Baker, Edinburgh

John Barclay, A. M. Edinburgh

Mr Peter Bathgate, weaver, Ayton

Mr Robert Baillie

Mr Robert Bowmaker, Chirnfide

Mr Robert Brown, coal owner, Wickham

Mr Michael Brown, Morpeth

Mr John Bonner, Stitchel (copies

Mr David Bonner, Woolwich, 2co

Mrs Beatrix Bonner, Auchencrow

C

Hon. John Campbell, Lord Stonefield, 2 copies

Alexander Chriftie, Efq; of Grueldykes, fheriff depute, Berwick-fhire

Duncan Campbell, Efq; fheriff fubftitute of Argylifhire

David Campbell, Efq; of Combie

John Campbell, Efq; of Auch

Ewen Cameron, Efq; of Fafsfern

William Cadell, Efq; of Banton

George Cadell, Efq; Edinburgh

James Carfrae, Efq; merchant, Edinburgh

James

James Clark, M. D. Newcaftle

Thomas Cleghorn, Efq; coachmaker, Edinburgh

B. Clifton, Efq; Edinburgh

T. S Conftantius, Efq;

Andrew Coventry, M. D. Profeffor of Agriculture, Edinburgh, 3 copies

William Creech. Efq; bookfeller, Edinburgh 24 copies

Thomas Curtis, Efq; Edinburgh

Captain John Cowe, Edinburgh

Reverend Mr Chalmers, Haddington

Reverend Mr William Chalmers, Auchtergaven

Mr Robert Campbell, fherriff clerk, Invernefs, 2 copies

Mr George Charlton, Newcaftle

Mr William Charnley, bookfeller, Newcaftle

Mr William Crawford, Edinburgh

Mr Robert Currie, apothecary, Newcaftle

D

Dowager Lady Dundas, of Kerfe, 2 copies

George Dempfter, Efq; of Dunnichen, 3 copies (copies

William Darnell, Efq; Newcaftle, 2

Reverend Thomas Davidfon, of Muirhoufe, D. D.

William Dawfon, Efq; Frogton 4 cop.

Captain Deans, of the Royal Navy, Huntington

James Donaldfon, Efq; printer, Edin.

Colin Drummond, M. D. Edinburgh

James Drummond, Efq; of Strageath

Keith Dunbar, Efq; Edinburgh

John Dyfon, Efq; glafs manufacturer, Newcaftle

Mrs Dirom, Queen Street, Edinburgh

Mrs C. Durham, George's Square, Edinburgh

Mr John Dennis, Newcaftle

Mr Thomas Dixon, Glafs-houfe, Newcaftle

Mr James Donaldfon, Dundee

Mr John Doxford, Morpeth

E

Thomas Elder Efq; of Forneth, Poftmafter General, and late Lord Provoft of Edinburgh

James Elliot, Efq; Queen Street, Edinburgh (3 copies

James Francis Erfkine, Efq; of Marr,

Reverend John Erfkine of Carnock, D. D. Edinburgh (pies

James Erfkine, Efq; of Cardrofs 2 co.

Methven Erfkine, Efq; of Cambo

Mr James Elder, fadler, Edinburgh

F

Honourable Archibald Frafer of Lovat, 5 copies

Colonel Ferrier, Edinburgh, Scotch Brigades

George Fairholme, Efq; of Greenknow.

Francis Farquharfon, Efq; of Oughton

William Fife, Efq; furgeon, Newcaftle

Captain John Forbes, royal navy

James Forman, Efq; W. S. Edinburgh (copies

Jofeph Forfter, Efq; of Setonburn 2

———— Forfter, M. D. Newtown of the Sea, Northumberland

James Frafer, Efq; of Gortuleg, W. S. Edinburgh

William Fullarton, Efq; (copies

Mr Thomas Fair, tenant, Refton, 2

Mr John Fellfhaw, of Southwell

Mr Fletcher, gardener, Reftalrig

G

Sir John Gordon of Invergordon. Bart.

Thomas

Thomas Gillespie, M. D. Edinburgh

Lewis Gordon, Esq; Depute Secretary of the Highland Society, Edin.

James Farquhar Gordon, Esq: Edinburgh

—— Gordon, Esq; W. S. Edinburgh

—— Gordon, Esq; Edinburgh

James Grant, Esq: of Corriemony, advocate

John Gray, Esq; W. S. Edinburgh

Reverend William Greenfield, D. D. Professor of Rhetoric, Edinburgh

James Grierson, Esq; of Dalgonerie 3 copies

George Grieve, M. D. Newcastle

Reverend Mr William Greig, Longside, Aberdeenshire

Mr Ebenezer Gairdner, merchant, Edinburgh

Mr Benjamin Gibson, Newcastle

Mr John Goldie, gardener

Mr Gordon, vintner, Press Inn

Mr William Grant, weaver's wright, Edinburgh

Mr Alexander Greenfield, portioner, Auchencrow

H

Sir James Hall of Dunglass, Bart. 3 (copies

Patrick Home, Esq; of Wedderburn, M. P. Berwickshire, 3 copies

William Hall, Esq; of Whitehall, 3 copies

Alexander Hamilton, M. D. Professor of Midwifery, Edinburgh

James Hamilton, M. D. Edinburgh 2 copies

James Hare, Esq;

Charles Hay, Esq; of Faichfield, advocate (copies

Robert Hay, Esq; of Drummelzier 10

James Horne, Esq; W. S. Edinburgh, 2 copies

George Home, Esq; of Branxton 4 copies

James Home, Esq; of Fairlaw (pies

P. Hunter, Esq; junior, of Thurston

James Huntly, Esq; surgeon, Gateshead, Newcastle.

Thomas Hutchison, Esq; merchant, Edinburgh

Mr Alexander Hutchison, merchant, Edinburgh

Rev. Mr William Haigh, Newcastle

Mr William Hall, Newcastle

Mr Robert Hay, wright, Edinburgh

Mr Thomas Henderson, Leith

Mr Peter Hill, bookseller, Edinburgh 6 copies

Mr John Hogg, merchant, Newcastle

I

Patrick Inglis, Esq; merchant, Edinburgh

—— Ingrame, M. D. Newcastle

John Innes, Esq; W. S. Edinburgh

Mr William Ingledew, Newcastle

J.

James Jackson, Esq; merchant, Edinburgh

John Jamieson, junior, Esq; Leith

—— Johnston, M. D. Dunbar

Reverend Mr J. Johnston, Alnwick

Mr William Johnston, Factor, Foulden

Mr Johnston, weaver, Newtown of the Muir

K

William Keith, Esq; accomptant, Edinburgh

—— Kentish, Esq; surgeon, Newcastle

Mr Thomas Kay, bookseller, Strand, London, 50 copies

L

William Leaviss, Esq; Newcastle

Edward Lothian, Esq; W. S. Edinburgh

Alexander Low, Esq; of Cash

Archibald

Jonathan Anderson Ludford, M. D.
Clarendon, Jamaica

Archibald Lundie, Efq; W. S. Edin.

Reverend Mr Henry Lundie, Edin.

Reverend Mr James Landels, Coldingham

Mr Herman Lyon, apothecary, E-
dinburgh

Mr George Lothian, merchant, Glaf-
gow

Mr William Lothian, merchant, E-
dinburgh

Mr Addifon Langhorn, Newcaftle

Mr M. Lofthoufe, Gatefhead, Newcaftle

Mr John Law, meffenger, Edinburgh

M

Right Honourable Robert M‘Queen
of Braxfield, Lord Juftice Clerk

Sir Alexander M‘Kenzie, of Coull,
Baronet, 2 copies

Alexander Monro, M. D. profeffor
of anatomy, Edinburgh

Mrs M‘Donald of Sanda

Mrs M‘Donald, of Clanronald, 2 cop.

Donald M‘Donald, Efq; of Kinloch-
moidart

Angus M‘Donell, Efq; of Auchtrichen

Donald M‘Intofh, Efq; writer, Edinburgh

John M‘Kenzie, Efq; W. S. Edinburgh

Captain M‘Kenzie, Royal Navy

Alexander M‘Kenzie, Efq; writer, E-
dinburgh

William M‘Leod, Efq; of Kaimes,
fheriff depute of Bute

John M‘Murdoch, Efq; Drumlanrick

Lauchlan M‘Tavifh, Efq; W. S.

R. Marjoribanks, Efq; Prince's Street,
Edinburgh

David Martin, Efq; limner, Edinburgh

Gilbert Meafon, Efq; of Mordun

George Midford, Efq; Morpeth

Archibald Milne, Efq; W. S. Edinburgh, 2 copies

William Molle, Efq; W. S. Ediburgh

Robert Moore, Efq; of Blairtown,
Ayrfhire, 2 copies

John Morthland, Efq; advocate, Edin.

James Wolfe Murray, Efq; advocate,
Edinburgh

Reverend Mr William M‘Ritchie,
Clunie

Reverend Mr Robert Mudie, Clack-
manan

Mr John Mackie, of Rora

Mr George Mowcy, Newcaftle

Mrs Maitland, Gayfield, Edinburgh

Mr Robert M‘Kay, manufacturer,
Berwick

Archibald M‘Kinlay, Efq; merchant,
Edinburgh

Mr Daniel M‘Queen, Sun-Fire-office,
Edinburgh

Mr Hugh M‘Whirter, Bleacher,
Inglefgreen   (copies

Mr George Mickle, Swinton Houfe, 2

Mr Moore, fchoolmafter, Morpeth,
6 copies

Mr Motlay, Morpeth

Meffrs George Mudie and Son, bookfellers, Edinburgh, 12 copies

Mr Andrew Muirhead, Edinburgh

Mr John Moir, printer, Edinburgh, 2
copies

N

John New, Efq;

William Newton, Efq; of Newton

Jofeph Norris, Efq; one of the clerks
of Jufticiary, Edinburgh

Mr James Normand, Edinburgh

O

John Ogilvy, Efq; of Gardoch,

Stephen

P

Stephen Pemberton, M. D. Newcastle

Reverend Mr James Playfair, Bendochy

Mr Samuel Paterson, merchant, Edinburgh

Mr James Pentland, merchant, Newcastle

Mr John Proctor, surgeon, Newcastle

Mr Peter Pae, merchant, Coldingham

Mr George Purves, Auchencrow

R

The Hon. David Rae, Lord Eskgrove

Sir Alexander Ramsay Irvine, of Balmain, Baronet

Peter Ramsay, Esq; younger of Barnton, banker, Edinburgh

J. Ramsay, M D. Newcastle, 2 cop.

David Ramsay, Esq; printer, Edinburgh

George Rennie, Esq; Linton   (copies

Alexander Renton, Esq; Lamberton, 6

John Robertson, Esq; Laurifton (burgh

Adam Rolland, Esq; advocate, Edin-

Adam Rolland, Esq; W. S. Edinburgh

Colin Rofs, Esq; of Caftlemilk

Matthew Rofs, Esq; advocate, Edin.

Walter Rofs, Esq; factor on the eftate of Cromarty, 2 copies

———— Rofs, Efq; of Kilmanivaig   2

Reverend Mr John Robertfon, Little Dunkeld

———— Redpath, M. D. Berwick, 2 cop.

Mr Charles Raitt, wood manufacturer, Newcastle

———— Reid, Efq; builder, Edinburgh

Mr Thomas Robfon, failer, Morpeth

Mr Robfon, fhip-builder, Newcaftle

Mr Thomas Robfon, wharfinger, Newcaftle

S

Right Hon. Sir James Stirling, Bart. Lord Provoft of Edinburgh (copies

Hon. David Smith, Lord Methven 2

Hon. John Swinton, Lord Swinton

Hon. Sir John Sinclair, of Ulbfter Bart. M. P. Prefident of the Board of Agriculture, &c. 7 copies

Hon. Lady Diana Sinclair, of Ulbfter

Hon. Lady Janet Sinclair, of Ulbfter

P Sandilands, Efq; Edinburgh

Dominico Felix Dos Santos, M. D. Brazil   (copies

William Scott, Efq; of Frierfhaw, 3

George Shadforth, Efq; Newcaftle

George Sinclair, Efq; merchant, Leith

Jofeph Smith, Efq; Meadow-houfe 2 copies

———— Sommerville, Efq; furgeon, Haddington 3 copies   (burgh

Andrew Stewart, Efq; W. S. Edin-

Charles Stewart, M. D. Edinburgh

Francis Strachan, Efq; W. S. Edinburgh

James Strachan, Efq; W. S. Edinburgh

Nathan Surgeon, Efq; furgeon, Newcaftle

Reverend Mr Sharp, Coldingham

Reverend Mr Shepherd, Bolam

Reverend Mr William Syme, New caftle

Mr Alexander Scott, Coldingham

Meffrs Thomas and William Sommers, vintners, Edinburgh

Mr Alexander Steel, merchant, Edinburgh

Mr Strange, teacher of dancing, Edinburgh

Mr Robert Swanfton, tenant, Newfarm

T

John Tawze, Efq; W. S. Edinburgh

Anthony Taylor, Efq; Infirmary, Newcaftle

J Thompfon, M. D. Gayfield, Edinburgh

Charles Thomfon, Efq; Edinburgh

Thomas Tod, Efq; Edinburgh

Thomas Tod, junior, Efq; George's Square, Edinburgh

Alexander

Alexander Tweedie, Efq; of Quarter

John Tweedie, Efq; writer, Edinburgh

Mr Robert Tweedie, merchant, Edinburgh

Reverend Mr Robert Trotter, Morpeth

Mr John Tait, joiner, Guyzon

Mr Thomas Taylor, Newburn

Mr Robert Thomfon, merchant, Edinburgh

Mr Andrew Thompfon, Lauder

Mr Thomas Thompfon, inn-keeper, Gatefide

Mr William Themfon, Haddington

Mr James Thorburn, grocer, Edinburgh

Mr Train, engraver, Bourdeau houfe

U

James Ure, Efq; Comptroller of the Cuftoms, Alloa

Reverend David Ure, A. M. Edinburgh

V

Cafpar Voght, Efq; Hamburgh

John Veitch, Efq; Surgeon, Ayton

W

Andrew Wardrop, Efq; furgeon, Edinburgh

John Wilfon, Efq; Morpeth

James Wood, M. D. Newcaftle

Mrs Alexander Wood, Edinburgh

George Wood, Efq; furgeon, Edinburgh

Reverend Mr Wilfon, Ayton

Mr. James Watfon, merchant, Newcaftle

Mr Walker, North America

Mrs Wardlaw, Edinburgh

Mrs Watfon, Charlotte Square, Edin.

Mr William Watfon, upholfterer, Edinburgh

Mr John White, fchoolmafter, Ayton

Mr Robert Whitfield, Morpeth

Mr Jofeph Whitfield, bookfeller, Newcaftle

Mr George Whitlaw, Ayton

Mr ------ Woodman, Morpeth

Y

Mr Ebenezer Young, bailie of Dunfe

Mr John Young, Edinburgh

A confiderable number of fubfcriptions, befides thofe above inferted, have been obtained for this work, which the author is forry he cannot infert, his correfpondents not having yet tranfmitted him their lifts.

CONTENTS

CONTENTS.

CHAP.

NEW

CHAP. I.

OF THE PLEASURE AND PROFIT, THAT ATTEND THE
KEEPING OF BEES.

BEES, thofe emblems of virtue, have long been the ftudy and delight of wife men, and have employed the ableft pens in many nations, and in different ages. In the facred writings, the land of Canaan is fpoken of as a good land, and, as an evidence of its being fo, it is called a land flowing with milk and *honey*. Among the ancients, Ariftomachus contemplated bees for the fpace of fifty-eight

A   years;

years; and Philiſcus retired into the woods, that he might have more convenient opportunities of obſerving them. Among the moderns, I ſhall juſt only mention Purchas, Rouſden, Geddie, Butler, Warder, Bradley, Thorly, Thomas and Daniel Wildman, Stephen and William White, and Keys, all Engliſhmen, and Robert Maxwell, a Scotchman;—all of whom have publiſhed treatiſes on them, the moſt of which have appeared within this century; and they have given many uſeful directions how to manage bees, according to the knowledge they had attained to, reſpecting that admirable inſect.

The knowledge of bees, like that of many other things, is found out by degrees, and may be ſaid, in ſome meaſure, to be ſtill but in a ſtate of infancy, as appears by the many miſtakes fallen into, and taught by thoſe who have wrote on that ſubject, notwithſtanding their fair promiſes in their title pages; as—" A Complete " Guide for the management of Bees," &c. They have all been ſtrangely miſled in their opinion about the generation of bees, aſſerting that the Queen lays three different kind of eggs, *viz.* one kind for the production of the Queen Bee, another for that of the Working Bees, and a third

third for the Drones ; an opinion, which the
author of the following sheets will, he humbly hopes, prove to be erroneous.

As in every undertaking there is some leading motive, which excites us to engage in it, so
the rearing of bees is attended with a degree
both of profit and pleasure, highly deserving
the attention of the philosopher, the gentleman-
farmer, and the industrious peasant. What
is more pleasant, than to observe the labours of
a hive of bees in the spring, when the days
begin to lengthen, and frost and snow, like
birds of darkness, cannot bear the sun ! Then
these industrious creatures begin to fly about,
and dance and sing, rejoicing at the return of
the genial season ! Then they reform what is
amiss in the hive, and, as their family en-
larges, they omit no opportunity of gathering
in fresh provision for their increasing young.
In the honey season, how delightful to see
them hurrying in their yellow loads ! How diligent they are to lay up provision for the returning winter ! View them in this smiling clover
field, or yonder flowery mead ! See how busily
they work ! And hear how sweetly they sing !
How pleasant to behold a swarm of bees light-
ly flying in the air, and darkening the heavens

with

with a thoufand varying lines ! Now, behold the innumerable tribe, formed into one compact body, fufpended from yonder verdant fhrub, eftablifhing themfelves into an independent colony, while their careful mafter, with confcious delight, meditates on his increafing ftore !

Bees, when properly managed, are alfo very profitable, as, in good years, moft hives will throw two fwarms; in moderate years, one. Although, in bad years, perhaps, fome will fwarm none at all, yet, eftimating by moderate years, and allowing each hive, one with another, to fwarm only once, which valuing at 15s. each, twenty ftock hives will thereby yield their mafter 15l. yearly;—no fmall fum to be got with fo much pleafure, and fo little toil. They will yield that much, although one or two fhould die in winter; nor need any think my eftimate too high ; if their hives be good, they will have that much one year with another. For example, in fummer 1787, the advantage arifing from bees was fuch, that many proprietors of them made 30s. and fome even 40s. of one fingle hive; and in March 1788, I fold a hive to a neighbour of mine, which in the following fum-

mer

mer increafed to five, four of which he fet afide
for ftock hives that autumn.

As there is no concern, in rural œconomy,
more profitable than bees, in favourable feafons, confidering the trifling expence that
attends them, we fhall here give an eftimate
to what extent bees may be reared, and alfo
what their value may amount to in ten years.

Suppofe, for inftance, one fhould begin with
five hives, which will coft him 5l., no great
fum to commence bee-mafter with, and allowing each hive, one with another, to double
their number, they will increafe in the following proportions :

Years.	Hives.
1	5
2	10
3	20
4	40
5	80
6	160
7	320
8	640
9	1280
10	2560

Thus,

Thus, in the fpace of 10 years, 5 hives will produce 2560 fwarms, which, valued at 10s. each hive, a very moderate eftimation, amounts to 1280l. clear profit; allowing the fecond and third fwarm to pay for hives, ftools, labour, and incidental loffes.

By the above calculation, my reader muft not conclude, that every hive of bees will produce fo many; but, I confidently affert, that many have done fo, and much more, in proportion, according to the time they have ftood; but, fuppofing 160 of thefe hives fhould fail by cold, robbers, famine, or bad management, during the above mentioned years, there will ftill remain 1200l. of clear profit.

Let it alfo be confidered here, that by the above eftimation, it is taken for granted, that the feafons are very favourable for bees, being fine, calm, funny warm weather, with foft fhowers now and then, and alfo plenty of good pafture in their neighbourhood, whereon they will work and fing without moleftation; wantonly fkipping from flower to flower, and rifling all their fweets, rejoicing that they are amply provided with fuch plenty of provifion, while the fmiling fun invites them to enjoy it. With what delight have I often witneffed my

                                        induftrious

induftrious fervants carrying on their work
with fo much fimplicity, alacrity, and chear-
fulnefs, and finging fo fweetly ; infomuch that
they are fit to make me join the concert, and
fing,

What's this I hear, makes fuch melodious found !
Surely I've got on fome enchanted ground.
'Tis Canaan's infects that I here behold,
Whofe legs do glitter like the yellow gold.
The furze and broom in luftre here do fhine,
Whofe yellow tops regale thofe flocks of mine.
Here filver ftreams in flow'ry valleys glide,
And rows of willows deck the river's fide :
Here lambkins play upon the funny braes,
And fweeteft nectar fmells on clover lees.
Here are the fields with Nature's colours dight,
Grateful to fmell, and pleafant to the fight.
Retired pleafure foothes and calms the mind ;
A noify world oft leaves a fting *behind.*

On the contrary, however, fhould the feafon
go to the other extreme, and, inftead of fair weather, fhould windy, cold, wet, cloudy, and heavy
weather take place, during fummer, the bees
will by it be fo much difheartened and difcouraged, that they will lament and mourn, in fo
piteous

piteous and diſconſolate a manner, that they have often made ſuch an impreſſion on my ſpirits, that I was fit to mourn along with them. The truth is, I have often thought that there was ſomething of the nature of a bee in myſelf; as always when they are happy, and rejoicing, ſo am I; when they are mourning and diſconſo-late, my ſpirits are alſo low; when fighting and plundering from one another, my temper is ſo chagrined, that it is with difficulty I re-ſtrain the effects of my ill humour; inſomuch, that my domeſtics, with little knowledge in phyſiognomy, can eaſily judge from the chear-fulneſs, depreſſion, or chagrin, apparent on my countenance, the ſtate and temper of my little republics.*

It

* A two-fold reaſon may be aſſigned for this. Fine weather enlivens the animal ſpirits, whereas a dull ſky, and a cloudy atmoſ-phere, generally produce the contrary effect. In the latter caſe, the bees can do nothing but conſume a part of that delicious ſtore, which they had laid up for their own and their maſter's uſe. Sympathy and intereſt are therefore equally excited, by ſuch weather, to produce this effect; and ſtill more by the circumſtance of their killing one another; for that man muſt be callous, indeed, to every feeling of humanity, who can, with indifference, behold numbers of ſuch uſeful and induſtrious animals, lying like ſo many murdered heroes on the field of battle, mutually ſlain by each o-ther; not to add, that a perſon of the moſt ſtoical diſpoſition muſt feel ſomewhat ruffled, at the loſs of ſo many uſeful ſervants, whom he would do every thing in his power to preſerve.

In fuch unfavourable feafons, bees increafe fo very little, that, perhaps, the owner can fcarcely collect, from among all his hives, as many good ones, as will keep up his ftock properly for the next feafon; but as fuch bad feafons does not happen often, it fhould not difcourage any perfon from commencing beemafter, as even, in the very worft, with proper care, the ftock may always be preferved, which is not the cafe with many other articles in which mankind deal.

It is hardly neceffary to obferve, that bees have amazingly thriven laft year, as almoft every hive produced twice, and many even thrice; and confequently, the price of honey has thereby been greatly reduced, from what it was in former years.

C H A P. II.

OF THE APIARY.

As a general rule, place your hives where they will be leaft expofed to the wind, and enjoy as much of the influence of the fun as poffible; for wind always retards the bees in their work,

B   while

while the fun's beams invite them to it. Although it is well known, that bees will thrive well in high and windy fituations, yet a low one is always to be preferred. In the neighbourhood of the apiary, there fhould be abundance of flowers, from which the bees may collect their wax and honey.

Were a choice allowed me, where to place my bees, it would be in an early fituation,—a hollow glen by the fide of a rivulet, furrounded with abundance of turnips in bloffom, in the fpring,—muftard and clover in fummer,—and heath in the latter end of fummer and harveft; with a variety of other garden and wild flowers in their feafons. However I would not be underftood, as if I hinted that bees would not thrive, unlefs they were placed in fuch an advantageous fituation, as the contrary can be proved: for bees have thriven amazingly well, in places where they were not within reach of many of the above mentioned flowers; but although they will do well in moft fituations, and fly far for food, yet they will thrive far better, when fituated among or near good pafture; and furrounded with abundance of food. This leads us forward to fhew what is the proper pafture for bees, which fhall be the fubject of the following chapter.

C H A P.

C H A P. III.

OF THE PASTURAGE, OR FLOWERS, PROPER FOR BEES TO FEED ON, WITH A CATALOGUE OF SOME OF THE PRINCIPAL ONES.

Among the great variety of flowers, which wife Nature has fo profufely laid before our noble infects, from which they may abundantly fupply themfelves with food, we fhall, in the firft place, give fome particular account of thofe five principal ones in this country, from which bees extract vaft quantities of honey;—viz. turnips, rape, muftard, clover and heath; and then conclude this chapter, with fome account of many other excellent flowers which bees feed on.

Turnips, in particular, blow early in the fpring, and continue long in flower; and they alfo yield both honey and farina, by which the bees are greatly excited to go abroad, and work upon them, when perhaps, in late fituations, they have fcarcely any other flower to

work

work upon. In fuch places, therefore, it is highly proper, that turnips be fowed, and allowed to remain in the ground during winter. Thefe, yielding their flowers from the middle of March to the end of April, will afford the bees fix weeks good pafture, and thus render them equal to thofe in more favourable or earlier fituations; whereas they would perhaps have fcarcely had any other flower to work upon, that could do them much good. I would therefore, ftrongly recommend to all proprietors of bees, particularly thofe in late fituations, if they can by any means, to let always as many turnips run into bloffom in the fpring, as may be fufficient to afford plenty of early pafture for their bees to work on. Thus the rich may fupply themfelves with that feed for fowing, and the poor will have it to fell to thofe who need it, which will enable them to pay the rent of the ground they grow upon. But here it may naturally be afked, By what rule are we to judge, what quantity of ground will yield a fufficiency of food for any given number of hives? I anfwer, that very little ground will keep many hives abundantly at work; as, for example, one acre of good land would not be overftocked with 20 hives; and confequently,

the

the twentieth part of an acre would keep one in constant employment.

The rape in blossom answers the same end to bees as the turnips; and as it is a little later of flowering, it will yield the bees a fresh and seasonable supply, when the turnips begin to fade, and thereby keep them constantly at work till the latter end of May, * when all the herbs of nature will, as it were, vie with each other who shall contribute most to supply this noble and virtuous race, with abundance of the sweetest nectar. Then, at this season, the balmy plane-tree regales them in the morning, before the drowsy herd ascends the hill to relieve his imprisoned bleaters: and the gold-like furze, mustard, and broom, invite them to feast till the day decline.

Garden and wild mustard, with runches of all kinds, bees are very fond of, and work keenly thereon; and these flowers are attended with this advantage, that by sowing their seeds at different times in the Spring, their flowering may

---

* The two flowers above mentioned, as they are easily raised, should be paid particular attention to, in the Highlands of Scotland, or any other Moorland situations, where there are very few natural flowers growing, except the heath.

may be fo protracted, as to afford the bees a
fufficiency of pafture during the whole working feafon.

In June comes the white clover, which continues long in bloffom, and alfo yields abundance of the fineft of honey: And wherever
the proprietor of bees has it in his power, he
fhould be particularly attentive to raife it in
his pafture lands; and, as I hinted with refpect
to turnips and rape, the clover grafs will
pay the rent of the ground, exclufive of what
advantage the bees derive from it. So fond
are the bees of this flower, that whenever it
appears, they will defert and overlook many
other excellent flowers, as unworthy of their
attention, and eagerly dart upon it, and work
and fing thereon all the day long, until the
cold evening chafe them with reluctance home
to reft: But, as all nature's beauties fade, and
thereby give way to their fucceffors, fo does
this beloved herb, as, about the end of July,
they begin to blacken, and the balmy dew to
forfake their fweeteft lips; then our heroes go
in fearch of frefh provifions, and in their ram-
bles, as they fkim over our lofty mountains,
are attracted by the blue heather bells, which
are numberlefs as the fands on the fea fhore;

each

each one of which, by the affiftance of Phœ-
bus, difclofes its fweets, and thereby invites
the tranfported bee to rifle all their charms.

Heath is attended with this advantage,
that it needs no culture nor rearing ; but, on
the contrary, grows fpontaneoufly, in too great
abundance, in many places ; as, moft certainly,
the greater half of Britain is covered with it ;
but, like the clover, it yields alfo vaft quantities of the fineft honey ; and, when the month
of Auguft is favourable warm weather, no
thriving hives of bees, placed near it, need
fail, in a fhort time, to enrich themfelves with
plenty of honey.

The flowers of furze, broom, and plane tree,
as formerly hinted, are highly grateful to bees,
as all of them afford abundance of matter to
collect their honey and wax from. Furze, in
particular, generally flowers early, and continues long in bloffom.

Befides the flowers above mentioned, there
is a great variety of others, which, in their different feafons, afford employment and materials for the bees ; fuch as lillies, rofe-marys, yellow
gowans, and the bloffoms of crocufes, fnow-
drops, oziers, fallows, vetches, alders, poppies,
beans, goofeberry bufhes, and fruit trees of all
kinds.

kinds. In fhort, I know no flower that they
will refufe, when they are at a lofs for variety ;
for, like the poor among mankind, when a
choice is denied them, they will be contented
with coarfe fare ; but give them their option
amongft a variety, and it will foon be perceived,
how little they value the gaudy *fhow*, when put
in competition with *fubftance ;* for they will fly
over the fineft gardens, and the moft beautiful
flowers, and cheerfully feed on their beloved
turnips, runches, clover, and heath.

There is one thing very obfervable, that
whatever flower a bee firft pitches upon, fhe
always continues to work upon the fame fpecies, till fhe is loaded, although fhe fhould be
obliged to fly over better kinds, and even to
fome confiderable diftance for them ; but, if
the bees cannot obtain a full loading from thofe
flowers which they prefer, they fometimes
make up the remainder from other flowers.

What the honey dew confifts of, is difputed
among the learned. According to the ancients,
it was an efflux of air, a dew which fell upon
flowers. The moderns fay, it is rather a per-
fpiration of the fineft particles of the fap in
plants,

plants, which, evaporating through the pores, afterwards condenfe upon the flowers *.

" The honey dew (fays Mr Key) is not a
" liquid depoſited by the air on the leavés of
" plants, as is generally fuppofed ; for then,
" like other dews or fogs, it would fall on,
" and adhere to, all forts of plants indifcrimi-
" nately ; whereas, it is found only on a *few*
" particular plants ; and on them but partial-
" ly, for the young leaves afford none.

" This fubftance is as tranfparent and as
" fweet as honey, and is, in fact, perfect ho-
" ney, attracted through the pores of the
" leaves, by a peculiar fultry heat ; particular-
" ly when reflected through clouds. Some-
" times it is found on the leaves in the form
" of little drops or globules. But, at other
" times, being more diluted by the greater
" moifture of the atmofphere, it covers the
" leaves, as though they were fpread with a
" fine fyrup.

" The time, in which thefe honey dews are
" generally found, is from the beginning of
" June to the middle of July. But it will
" vary, in proportion as the weather is wet or

C   " dry;

* Nature Delineated.

" dry; which will occasion them to be either
" sooner or later. The hottest and driest sum-
" mers produce the largest and most frequent
" honey dews. In cold and wet seasons, few
" or none of them are to be seen.

" Whenever a honey dew is found, the bees
" are so extremely eager to fetch it, that they
" quit all other work, that their returns may be
" the quicker and more numerous; and lest a
" gloomy change should deprive them of the
" precious prize. No harvest swain, dreading
" impending storms, can be more anxious or
" expeditious, in hastening the housing of his
" crops, than these aerial tribes in this their
" delightful office; so much so, that thronging
" in too great numbers at the door, they
" jostle and tumble each other down. And
" smarting woe to those who shall thoughtless-
" ly stand in their way at this important cri-
" sis! Their joy on these occasions, is ex-
" pressed in such incessant and loud notes, as
" to be heard at a great distance. By these to-
" kens it may be known, that there is a honey
" dew, without seeing the trees from which
" they gather it."

A friend informed me, that he has often
discovered both bees and ants upon the oak

leaves

leaves, fipping the honey dew; which agrees
nearly with the Abbe Boissier de Sauvages's account of it, in France, as quoted
by Wildman, p. 80, et feq. For my part,
although I have often travelled many miles, in
the fineft weather, to places where oaks were
growing in great abundance, in order to fatisfy myfelf on that point, yet I never could
difcover a fingle drop of honey dew on them,
or any bees to collect it. And many perfons
have affured me, that they never faw a fingle
bee upon an oaken leaf collecting honey. I
am, neverthelefs, far from difcrediting the report; as thofe who are fituated nearer extenfive woods, have doubtlefs much better opportunities of afcertaining this fact, than I. And
that there are honey dews to be difcovered in
fuch fituations, I readily believe; as I have often obferved my own bees collecting honey
from the *outfides* of the fockets of different
flowers, particularly from thofe of the wild
runches, inftead of extracting it by their probofcis from the *infide*. I have fometimes,
though very feldom, obferved them, in a fine
morning, about fun-rife, bufily employed upon
the leaves of the white thorn, at a feafon
when there was not a fingle flower to be feen

C 2   on

on it ; which inclines me to think it is not an *efflux of air*, as some suppose, but rather a perspiration of some of the finest particles of the sap of plants, which, evaporating through the pores, afterwards condenses upon the leaves. At such favourable opportunities, the bees will doubtless soon fill their hives with honey ; but I am of opinion, that such happy seasons are generally very short, and that for many years they last but a very few days ; and in some cold years, perhaps they scarcely occur at all.

Some writers believe, that when the liquor which the bees collect, has been for some time in their stomachs, it comes from thence changed into true honey ; the liquor having been there properly digested, and rendered thicker than when it entered. Others are of opinion, that the bee makes no alteration in the honey, but collects this delicious syrup just as nature produces it, and first fills her bag, and then discharges it into the magazine ; which appears to me to be the most probable opinion ; as I have sometimes taken a bee from a flower the moment she was collecting the honey, and torn her asunder, (although with the greatest reluctance,)

reluctance,) to satisfy myself on that point; when
I found the finest *blob* of honey in her bladder,
exactly of the fame tafte, colour and fmell,
with that honey which is ufually collected
from fuch flowers as the bee was working u-
pon; for thofe bees which I picked off the
white clover, contained fine white tranfpar-
rent honey, while fuch as were taken from
heath, produced it of a high colour; and as
the honey had not been above a minute in
their bladders, it certainly could not undergo
any change in fo fhort a fpace of time. But
even allowing the bees their own ufual time to
collect, carry home, and depofit the honey in
their cells, the time will be found not to exceed five minutes; and yet the honey is, at
this period, in as great perfection, nay, rather
better, if there is any difference, than at any
time thereafter: for it is proved by experience,
and acknowledged by all connioffeurs in apiaries, that the younger the honey and honey-comb
are, they are fo much the fairer and better;
as, when they remain for fome time in the
hive, the combs, by the breath of the bees, gradually become of a darker colour, and the
honey becomes neither fo fair nor fo tranfpar-
rent,

rent, as when it was first collected*. From all
which considerations, it appears plain to me,
that bees are not the makers of honey, but only collectors of it; and that the honey is in as
great perfection in the flowers, before the bees
touch it, if not better, than it is after it has paf-
sed through their bodies. †

* The author would not be underftood here, as if he meant
that honey fuddenly underwent a change to the worfe, as it will
remain many months locked up in the hives without undergoing
any material change; yet, neverthelefs, it is certain, that honey
is never better, than when it is newly depofited in the cells.

† Some alledge, that the fyrup in the flower, by paffing
though the body of the bee, undergoes a material change, and
is thereby converted into real honey. But there is no analogy
between the honey extracted by the bee, to be carried home to
the hive, and the meant or drink taken into the ftomach by any
other animal, to be digefted for its nourifhment. The former is
retained in the bladder of the bee only a few minutes; whereas, the latter continues many hours, and, by the operation of
the gaftric fluid, is changed into chyle, blood, &c. The honey
itfelf, when taken afterwards by the bees for the purpofe of
nourifhment, undergoes a fimilar change; but, in its firft ftate,
when put into the cells, it has undergone no change whatever.

I was this day favoured with a letter from a very intelligent
gentlemen, whofe opinion, on this fubject, although quite different from my own,—I fhall prefent to my reader.

" Honey does not exift in the plant in that form, but only be-
" comes fo by paffing through the body of the bee. While it
" is in the flower, it conftitutes what is called its faccharine
" juice

From the above reasoning we may conclude, that every single *heather bell*,* or cup of any other flower, is a vessel containing some of the finest honey, and that nothing in nature is a-wanting to make our land flow with it, and thereby enable both rich and poor to feast up-on it always at their pleasure.

A conjecture may naturally arise here, that, seeing bees do not *make* honey, but only col-lect it, if we could, by any device, fall upon a plan to extract it from the flowers; or, in o-ther words, to pour 10,000 of Nature's vessels full of honey into one of our artificial ones, it would be astonishing what a prodigious quan-tity might be produced throughout the island.

Scotland

" juice, and, when sucked up by the insect, is changed by the
" action of its vessels into honey.

" In proof of this assertion, take a number of hungry bees, and
" give them a full *meal* of sugar, diluted in water, tear one of
" them asunder immediately after, and its bladder will be found
" full of honey ; now, if sugar is so quickly converted into that
" form, have we any reason to doubt that the juice of the flower
" will undergo a change equally quick by the same means?

" I have often made this experiment, and the result has been
" uniformly the same. If the bee has made a meal of white su-
" gar, the honey found in its body is white ; if it has got brown
" sugar or triacle, the honey will be brown."

* Flower of heath.

Scotland alone, I will venture to affirm, would, in such a case, produce more honey and wax, in one good season, than would load one of his Majesty's first rate men of war. But as, hitherto, no such method has been discovered, and perhaps any such attempt would prove fruitless, let us study to increase, as quickly as possible, the number of those *natural chemists,* our valuable, faithful, and industrious servants, the BEES, who are every way qualified for the important task : having an exquisite smell to direct them to the flowers containing the nectarine juice,—a *proboscis,* or sucking tube, to enable them to extract it,—a reservoir to contain it,—wings to carry it away,—and fine clean vessels of their own manufacture to treasure it up in. And let us ever deprecate the barbarous practice of destroying such valuable creatures, who seem designed by Nature to work indefatigably for the benefit of mankind* ; and therefore

---

* We cannot more strongly express our detestation of the barbarous, and too general practice of smoaking hives, than in the beautiful and energetic language of the immortal Thomson :

> Ah, see where robb'd, and murder'd, in that pit
> Lies the still heaving hive ! at evening snatch'd,
> Beneath the cloud of guilt concealing night,

And

therefore, inftead of death and extirpation, merit every encouragement and prefervation ; and
ought, at leaft in autumn, to be allowed to re-
tain a reafonable fhare of the fruits of their
own induftry, to preferve them through the
D winter

And fix'd o'er fulphur : while, not dreaming ill,
The happy people in their waxen cells,
Sat tending public cares, and planning fchemes
Of temperance, for Winter poor ; rejoiced
To mark, full flowing round, their copious ftores.
Sudden the dark oppreffive fteam afcends ;
And, uf'd to milder fcents, the tender race,
By thoufands, tumble from their honeyed domes,
Convolv'd, and agonizing in the duft.
And was it then for this you roam'd the Spring,
Intent from flower to flower ? for this you toil'd
Ceafelefs the burning Summer-heats away ?
For this in Autumn fearch'd the blooming wafte,
Nor loft one funny gleam ? for this fad fate ?
O Man ! tyrannic lord ! how long, how long,
Shall proftrate Nature groan beneath your rage,
Awaiting renovation ? When obliged,
Muft you deftroy ? Of their ambrofial food
Can you not borrow ? and, in juft return,
Afford them fhelter from the wintry winds ;
Or, as the fharp year pinches, with their own
Again regale them on fome fmiling day ?
See where the ftony bottom of their town
Looks defolate, and wild ; with here and there
A helplefs number, who the ruin'd ftate
Survive, lamenting, weak, caft out to death.

winter and fpring ; whereby they will be enabled greatly to increafe in numbers, as well as
in produce, in the courfe of the fucceeding feafon.

In the next chapter we fhall take a view of
the vaft increafe of the number of hives that
may eafily be made in Scotland ; an object
which I am happy to find already begins to
occupy the attention of many gentlemen of
property ; and the promotion of which I hope
will foon become general. Nothing indeed
would yield me greater pleafure and fatisfaction, than if, by any exertion of mine, I could
be inftrumental in fetting on foot, or carrying
into execution, a meafure of fo much utility
and importance to the public.

C H A P. IV.

REASONS WHY THERE ARE SO FEW BEE-HIVES IN SCOTLAND.

IT is not to be expected, upon my propofed
plan, that I fhould enter deeply into the nature, generation, and properties of bees ; although

though each of these subjects might afford an investigation equally useful and interesting. On such subjects, I have often thought, I could write a thoufand pages, and, after all, be far from exhausting my thoughts on them. But, without diving deep at prefent into them, or entering the lists of controverfy with other authors, who have wrote upon them, my chief defign in this treatife was—

To excite men of property, who are the only proper perfons to be addreffed on the bufinefs, to exert themfelves with fpirit and perfeverance to promote the increafe of bee-hives in this country, by convincing them, that the cultivation of bees is an important object to the nation at large as well as to every proprietor of them.

To fhow, that the prices of HONEY and WAX would be thereby greatly reduced, and confequently thefe articles would become a fource of national wealth; and

That Britain, inftead of expending large fums of money in purchafing thefe articles from foreign countries, might even be enabled to render them an article of exportation; and therefore that they merit the attention of every patriot and real friend to his country. Alfo,

To

To show those who incline to make the attempt, how to proceed in such a laudable undertaking.

To give a brief account of the bee, as divided into its different classes of Queen, Drones, and Working bees ; and to conclude with

Some plain and easy directions, how to manage that useful and industrious race, through the different seasons of the year, so as they may prove of the greatest advantage to the country at large, as well as to their proprietors.

The principal reason, why bees have not been reared in greater numbers in this country, is, the almost total neglect of them, by gentlemen of property ; who seem, in general, to act as if they thought these useful insects entirely below their notice ; and the rearing and increasing of bee-hives, as a business so very insignificant, as to be unworthy of their patronage. Hence many gentlemen will rather purchase honey at the highest rate, than give themselves the trouble of rearing bees ; which neglect often likewise proceeds from an erroneous idea entertained by many, that bees will not thrive with them, and therefore the attempt would be fruitless. *

It

* Perhaps, in former ages, bees may have been more plentiful in
Scotland,

It is not the want of proper pasture, that prevents bees from thriving well every year in this country. The only preventative is the inconstancy of the weather; for if it be windy, or cloudy, they will not go out of the hive; and, on the other hand, though the day should be quite dry, yet if the weather be cold, the bees will collect very little honey.

From all the above mentioned causes, therefore, it is plain, that the bees and the bee-master, have nothing so adverse to their interest as the mutability of the weather; and the worst of the matter is, that nothing can be done to remedy this evil. Only the proprietor, by having plenty of good pasture at all seasons, has this advantage, that whatever good weather occurs between February and September, he may have his bees so well supplied with good flowers,

Scotland, than they have been for a considerable time past. This appears probable from different places still bearing their names from these useful animals. For instance, in my own native parish of Coldingham, there is a steeding called *Bee-Edge*, another named *Bee-Park*, and a rivulet denominated *Bee-Burn*. All these places have evidently derived their names from large quantities of bees having been formerly reared in them; as they are situated on the skirts of a large common, which is now divided, and where bees would still thrive well with proper care and attention, if the proprietors would exert themselves to render these places worthy the names they bear.

flowers, as that they shall be enabled to make the most of it, and to collect honey (as his hay-makers make hay,) while the sun shines. Here it may be observed, that bees will thrive well, and collect a good quantity of honey in a short time, if they only have three favourable days in the week, during the honey season; as a good hive, in thirty fine days, will collect four pints of honey : besides, many people will al-ledge, that their situation is too cold, windy, or rainy, with many other reasons, which in fact are of no weight; for the principal reason of bees not thriving is bad weather; and the next chief cause is the neglecting to take pro-per care of them. Their bees indeed will some-times thrive long and well, with very little care, which leads their proprietor to entertain an er-roneous idea, that they always will do so, and that hardly any care is necessary. But when cold, famine, or robbing bees attack his hives, and destroy his stock of bees, the lazy proprie-tor regrets his mistake when it is too late.

I believe poor people, in general, make more by their bees annually, than those in more af-fluent circumstances ; and even the latter might make far more of them than they do, if they would only study to increase their stock to a considerable confiderable extent. The reafon is, that they are a kind of *eftate* to the poor, who, when once they enter upon the bufinefs of rearing bees, take a great pleafure in it, and, by paying proper attention to them, gradually acquire more and more knowledge in the profeffion. And, the only reafon why fuch perfons do not increafe their ftock of hives, to a much greater number than the country at prefent poffeffes, is, that pinching poverty obliges them often to fell the beft of their hives for ready money, to make up their houfe rent: Not to add, that fuch perfons, when obliged to leave their cottages, owing to raifed rents, monopolies of farms, or the like, think bee-hives a very troublefome fpecies of property for removal. Befides, as they keep but a few hives each, they never think of raifing any flowers for provifion to them. And if a perfon in fuch circumftances fhould lay out 20 s. for a hive, and fhe prove a bad one and die, he and fome of his neighbours will perhaps ever after look upon the culture of bees as a dangerous and precarious adventure, not to be attempted by any but perfons in affluence. To obviate fuch objections, fhall be the fubject of the following chapter.

CHAP.

CHAP. V.

REASONS FOR, AND PRACTICABILITY OF, INCREASING THE
NUMBER OF BEE-HIVES IN SCOTLAND.

A NY perfon, who confiders how very abundantly Scotland is fupplied by nature, with
food proper for bees, throughout almoft every
county in the kingdom, and obferves how very few bees are reared, notwithftanding thefe
great advantages, muft be furprifed that fo
little exertion has hitherto been, made in that
line.   For inftance, were we to confider, that
fome parifhes, which might abundantly maintain 300 hives in each of them, have not at
prefent 20 or 30, we muft be furprized at that
infatuation which has hitherto prevented us
from attending more to our own intereft.
Were we to confider our large extended heath-
covered moors, and beautiful clover fields, with
the great quantities of runches, wild muftard,
&c. that grow fpontaneoufly in our corn fields,

together

gether with the many elegant gardens, nurferies, &c. raifed by art, in the neighbourhood
of this metropolis, and almoſt every other town
in Scotland, as well as the country feats of our
gentry, together with thofe numerous wild flowers that grow in our meadow grounds and
pafture lands, we might juftly fay, " the HAR-
" VEST truly is GREAT, but the LABOURERS
" are FEW."

And here I fhall mention a thought, which
ftruck me lately in a gentleman's garden, and
indeed has often ftruck me in fimilar fituations ;—" Here I am furrounded with a variety of fine flowers, and the profpeѐt all a-
round me is equally pleafant and delightful !
What a variety of Nature's beauties and fweets
are here exhibited, and how many thoufands
of millions of fockets of flowers there are, in
the vaſt number of gardens in this metropolis
and its environs !—and yet, the infatuated inhabitants and proprietors rather allow the
honey contained in thefe beautiful veffels to
be wafted, than employ a few of thofe faithful fervants, provided by nature, to extraѐt
and colleѐt it for them :—Servants, who would
chearfully labour, without wages, and find
themfelves in food and cloathing during their

employment, if the proprietor would only provide them a few fmall lodgings. Will thefe people ftill rather be at the expence of purchafing honey from me, or others, at a high rate, than rear hives to manufacture it for themfelves? Will they continue to fend their money to Dantzick, for honey of a far inferior quality, rather than encourage the produce of it at home?—Why do not the gentry of Edinburgh and the neighbourhood, efpecially thofe who live in the confines of the city, replenifh their gardens and nurferies with fome hundreds of hives, which they are fo well able to fill?" Similar reflections have cften ftruck my mind, when I have feen extenfive fields, abounding with white clover and heath, where the flowers, like the ftars of heaven, or the fand on the fea fhore, could be numbered not by units, tens, hundreds, or thoufands, but by *millions* !—Suppofe, for example, 1 fquare yard of heath or clover to contain 500 cups of flowers, each one of which contains fome honey, what an immenfe number would be contained in an extent of 6 fquare miles?

Some however here may reply, that a field may be overftocked with bees, as well as with fheep or black cattle. I will grant that there

is

is a poffibility of this, but I will venture to affirm, that fuch a thing has feldom ever yet happened in Britain*. Or, at leaft, if there is, or
ever was, any one place in the ifland overftocked with them, there are twenty other places, which never reared the fourth part of
the number that they were able to maintain.
Nay, there are many excellent fituations for
bees, which perhaps never had 20 ftock hives
on them, although by nature abundantly provided with excellent pafture for many hun-
E 2 dreds.

---

* There are fome few places, indeed, fuch as white benty
ground, where there is fcarcely a heath, clover, muftard, or
runch flower to be feen, nor even any furze, broom, or plane
trees growing, and which are almoft quite void of all other flowers. Such places are certainly very bad fituations for bees, and
they will never thrive on them, or on any fimilar unproductive
grounds. There are again fome other places, which have but a
few natural flowers, and where no artificial ones are reared. Such
places may perhaps have hardly a fufficient quantity of flowers in
eight miles circumference, to feed eight ftocks of hives ; Whereas, in more favourable fituations, the fame extent of ground
could eafily produce as many flowers as would feed eight fcore.
There are fome other grounds, which are excellent for producing corn, but which perhaps have little clover, muftard, or runches, in their neighbourhood, and neither gardens nor moors within reach. Such places are naturally bad fituations for bees ; but
by rearing fome turnips, muftard, or clover, and fome furze in
hedges, or on wafte grounds, they may eafily be rendered excellent fituations for thefe ufeful infects.

dreds. For, as has been often mentioned, when we confider the vaft quantity of flowers, which the earth naturally produces, and which might be ftill much more increafed by art, how prodigioufly great may we eftimate the total? This confideration may convince us of the little danger we have of running into the extreme of overftocking our fields with bees.

Some may perhaps alledge, that if there were twenty times more hives in Scotland than there are at prefent, the produce, in a bad feafon, would ftill be very trifling : But this is a very childifh objection ; for, even in the worft of feafons, the quantity of honey produced, would, by proper care and attention, ftill be twenty times greater than, in fuch a feafon, it is at prefent. For inftance, were there but one hive in all Scotland, in a cold rainy fummer ; even that hive would produce but a very fmall increafe, perhaps fwarm only once, and that fwarm produce but only one pint of honey ; whereas, if there are 100 hives, granting the weather to be equally bad, the produce muft be at leaft 100 pints of honey. Eftimating the number of parifhes in Scotland, capable of raifing bees, to be only 800, which I think is below the truth, the following calculation will give a view

of

of the immenfe quantity of honey that might be produced, even in ordinary favourable years.

	Hives.		*Pints of Honey.*
Suppofing, (which is moderate)	1	to produce	4
Then 1 hive in each parifh -	800	produces	3,200
Suppofing the number in each parifh increafed to 30, -	24,000	will produce	96,000
But fuppofing, (which is ftill very moderate) the number in each parifh increafed to 100 - - -	80,000	will produce	320,000
Suppofing the number in each parifh increafed to 400 -	320,000	will produce	1,280,000

			lbs. of wax.
Befides wax, which at 1lb. each hive, is		- -	80,000

But there are many parifhes in Scotland fo very large and extenfive, and fo full of rich flowers, that I believe 1000 hives erected in each of them, would not contain bees fufficient to extract the one half of the honey contained in their flowers, in favourable weather; and therefore, it would not be eftimating the poffible increafe of honey, all over Scotland, too high, to ftate it at near 2,000,000 of pints of honey. For example, the parifh in which I refide, was fo richly provided laft year with abundance of fine white clover, wild muftard, and heath flowers, &c. that 1500 hives of bees, placed properly on it, would not have nearly exhaufted

exhaufted its flowers of their honey.   To what an aftonifhing extent then might the bee-hufbandry be carried ? *

But left I fhould be thought extravagant, in my calculations and ftatements of the profits to be made from thefe ufeful animals, and inclined to lead my readers to build *caftles in the air*, inftead of erecting hives in their gardens, I fhall mention a few facts out of many on this fubject, which I can vouch, either from my own concern in them, or upon the authority of perfons with whom I am particularly acquainted, and who informed me how much they had made of their bees laft feafon.

To a perfon near Greenlaw, I
  paid for honey and wax, a-
  bove,   -   -   -   L. 4   0   0
To another near Dunfe, for
  ditto, above,   -   -   11   0   0
To another, near Hamilton, I
  paid for *one hive*, which was
  weighed in the Edinburgh
  Weigh-houfe,   -   -   4   0   0

For

---

* But it is neceffary to caution the reader here, that, in a very bad feafon, it perhaps could do little more than produce the fourth part of that quantity ; not for want of abundance of flowers with honey in them, but for want of favourable weather for them to go and collect it. See pages 7, 9 and 29.

For 40 hives, purchaſed from
  different perſons, ſome of
  them at above 2l. Sterling
  each, I paid   -   -   70 0 0
A friend in Mid-Lothian aſ-
  ſured me, he had cleared laſt
  ſeaſon, by his bees, no leſs
  than   -   -   -   12 0 0

All of theſe perſons had but a very few
ſtock hives at Whitſunday, and yet they made,
at an average, above 30s. by each of their hives.
But had they increaſed their ſtock, they might
eaſily have made ten times more than they
did.

With regard to the profit ariſing from bees,
one conſideration ſhould not be overlooked,
viz. that almoſt the whole produce, ariſing from
the ſale of both honey and wax, is in a great
meaſure clear proſit; as bees, and bee-hives
are, particularly in Scotland, equally free from
rents and taxes; and the culture of them does
not in the leaſt injure or impede any other improvement, in any reſpect. Nor do they require a conſtant attendance, as moſt other articles of improvement do; for a proper perſon
might eaſily overſee, with a little aſſiſtance in
ſwarming time, at leaſt 500 bee-hives. And

as

as Nature has amply fupplied them with food, and with powers to provide it for themfelves, they put their owners to little or no expence for that article; which cannot be faid of any other of our fervants whatever.*

Thus, by following the above plan, with a little attention and exertion on the part of our landed gentlemen, fuch a number of bee-hives would foon be raifed all over the kingdom, that

---

* Here I have in view Scotland in general, as it has many hundreds of fituations where bees would thrive well, but where not a fingle flower is fown for that purpofe; but even were this plan adopted, of rearing artificial flowers in thofe places, where a fcarcity of natural flowers prevails, during part of the working feafon, in order to fupply that defect, and thus afford the bees abundance of provifion at all times, ftill the expence would be fo trifling, that it is fcarcely worth taking notice of; as is already hinted, p. 12, &c. for, fhould we plant fome trees, with a view to affift bees, we have their wood; if we rear turnips, we have their feed; if we fow white clover, we have the beft of pafture; and if we even allow furze or broom to overfpread wafte grounds, we can be at little lofs, as even thefe have alfo their ufes, by fupplying us with hedging, fuel, fhelter for fheep, &c. I wifh not to be here underftood, as if I meant to recommend the fowing of large fields purpofely with food for bees, excepting white clover, which provides food for larger animals: All that I intend is, that gentlemen, who have great ftocks of bees, and plenty of ground, may eafily fpare three or four acres, out of as many hundreds, for the rearing of turnips, muftard, furze, broom, &c.

that the quantity of honey and wax would be increafed to fuch an extent, as to produce the greateft advantages to the nation at large, as well as to the private proprietors of the hives. All the money fent to foreign markets for thefe commodities would be kept at home; which would be a faving of perhaps not lefs than 50,000l. a-year. And honey would be produced in fuch abundance at home, as to fupply the poor, as well as the rich, not only with a delicious *luxury*, but alfo with an excellent fubftitute for fome *neceffaries*.

It might, for inftance, be converted into *mead*, a fine well-tafted wholefome liquor, which would prove an excellent fubftitute for ftrong ale and porter, and could be fold at a very moderate price. A weaker kind of mead, called *bragwort*, could alfo be made of it. This is an agreeable wholefome liquor, much efteemed by many, who ufe it as a fubftitute for fmall beer. When properly made, it will keep long: And when of a proper degree of ftrength, it is fo highly exhilarating, that many perfons have been fent home half intoxicated with it.

The increafe of the quantity of honey would alfo reduce the price of it fo much, that in-

ftead

stead of paying 1od. or 1s. *per* pound for it, as at present, it might be sold so low as 3d. *per* pound, in which case it would prove an excellent substitute for butter to the poor. E-ven at the present prices, it is already used by many persons mixed with butter.

As to the wax, almost every person knows the great uses made of that article, in medici-nal preparations, wax candles, sealing wax, &c. &c. as well as the high esteem in which wax candles and wax tapers, are held by persons in the higher ranks of life, on account of their clear light and odoriferous smell, as well as their freedom from all danger of greasing any thing, as tallow candles do, when a drop falls from them.

C H A P.

C H A P. VI.

HOW TO INCREASE THE NUMBER OF BEE-HIVES IN A FEW
YEARS IN SCOTLAND.

I PROCEED next to fhow, in what manner the number of bee-hives may be fpeedily encreaf- ed in Scotland. If a gentleman of property has a proper fituation for bees, and the above reafoning has inclined him to commence the cultivation of bees with fpirit, let him apply to fome perfon tolerably fkilled in that branch of fcience, and let him purchafe 100 or more bee-hives, in the month of Auguft, and place them properly, according to the directions which fhall be laid down hereafter. Let him next rear a fufficiency of turnips in their neigh- bourhood, that they may bloffom next fpring; and in the month of February, let him fow fome muftard feed, and fome furze and broom upon dykes, or wafte ground. Gentlemen of property, who have any ground proper for planting, fhould by all means plant a number of plane trees and fallows. They fhould like-wife fow a good deal of white clover, fweet refida, or mignionette, &c. with any other flowers that will grow upon the ground, either by nature or art.

In winter, particular care fhould be taken to preferve the bees from cold; in fpring, from famine, and robbery by other bees. And when they are ready to fwarm, great care muft be taken to lodge them in proper habitations.

With fuch attentive management, I can venture to affure all who will make the experiment, that 100 well-chofen ftock-hives, will, in a tolerably good feafon, produce from 180 to 200 or even 220 hives, whatever more.

Some may object, that, while the proprietor, who wifhes to increafe the breed of bees, raifes many flowers for that purpofe, his neighbour, who, perhaps, takes no trouble of this kind, may fhare the benefit, by his bees coming and feeding upon them §. To this it

may

---

§ I was fent for on the 23d of May laft, by a gentleman in Edinburgh, who wifhed me to bring him a hive of bees, and to pitch upon the moft proper fituation for placing it in his garden. The day being very fine, and the fruit trees in full bloffom, there was a pear tree among many others, which was full of fine bloffoms: Obferving a number of bees bufily employed upon them,

be fufficient to reply, that the induftrious proprietor, having done every thing in his power to
fupply

them, he told me, " they belonged to his *neighbour*, who lived
" a few yards from him."—" Perhaps not," replied I, " for a
" bee will fly far for food in fine weather : and, therefore, thefe
" bees may come from Leith, or fome other place as far diftant,
" while your neighbour's bees may fly as far as Leith for their
" loading."

As for the reafon why bees will fometimes travel a mile or
more for a heavy loading, when they could get the fame quantity and equally good, from the fame fpecies of flowers within a
few yards, I can fcarcely hazard a conjecture ; unlefs it be, that
perhaps fome of the old and experienced bees, from a miftaken
apprehenfion, may fuppofe thofe flowers near their hives to have
been exhaufted, by the moft part of the hive having had conftant
accefs to them, and feeding on them ; as is faid of the old cattle,
that they commonly feed on the borders of their pafture grounds,
where few of the younger cattle have previoufly fed. But, as a
proof of the fact, let any perfon who has one or two hives, with a-
bundance of flowers to keep his bees conftantly employed, within
100 yards of their hives, make the experiment, by going to another place, where there are alfo flowers growing 1000 yards diftant from his own, or any other perfons bees, and he will find a
great number of bees at work on the diftant flowers.

But though fome bees, by being expeditious travellers, feem to
difregard diftance, and to be fond of undertaking long journeys
even when loaded, yet, in general, I believe, the greater part
of them are wife enough to collect their loading as near their
hives as poffible. And, therefore, the nearer the flowers are fituated, the more work will they perform, and the greater quantity of honey will be carried home in a day. For this reafon, I
have already advifed the hives to be always placed as near as
poffible to plenty of provifions.

fupply his own bees with ample provifions, will
have the pleafure to fee them feed and thrive
upon it; and fhould thofe of his neighbours
occafionally partake, he will not have any reafon to regard it, there being no danger of a
famine. But to obviate this objection completely, let ten (or more) perfons in a village,
or neighbourhood, join together and contribute
equally in proportion to the number of their
hives, to rear a fufficient quantity of flowers a-
mongft them, and upon this amicable plan, the
expence of each proprietor will be exactly in
proportion to the number of his hives.

Suppofing, that there are, in May 1795,
twenty ftock hives in each parifh in Scotland,
the amount in 800 parifhes would be 16,000.
Then, fuppofing each of thefe hives to throw
one fwarm, which would probably keep through
the winter, in September we would have 32000
ftock hives. At this period, let every gentleman, who rears bees, keep all his hives, young
and old, for ftock hives, that are fit for it*:

Let

---

* All ftocks, or firft fwarms, and even fome fecond fwarms, will
probably anfwer for that purpofe ; and all fwarms which are nearly full of combs. but rather light, fuch as I would not advife to be
kept, if they were not fpeedily to increafe the ftock ; by keeping
them

Let the poor, who are able, do the fame with theirs ;—and let thofe, who are not able to lie out of the produce of their bees, fell them to thofe who are inclined to purchafe them for ftock hives. By doing this, they will raife as much honey as if they killed all the bees, and fold the honey and wax†, and with far lefs trouble.

On thefe principles, by keeping 32,000 ftock hives, with proper management, during a tolerable feafon, and always preferving all that will preferve, for the fpace of feven years, the ftock would increafe as follows : viz,

HIVES.

them, and feeding carefully with courfe honey, which might be purchafed from any foreign market, where it could be got at the cheapeft rate. For this purpofe, two or three very light fwarms, which are not fit to be kept for ftocks feparately, might, by conjoining both bees and honey, form a good ftock hive. And all hives, containing honey or combs, whofe bees defert them from whatever caufe, during any feafon of the year, might be kept carefully, to lodge new fwarms next feafon. The method of uniting, feeding, &c. will be defcribed in their proper places ; and by following the directions laid down under thefe heads, our hives would in a fhort time turn out very numerous.

† But fhould it here be afked, How are we to be fupplied with honey during the time of rearing the ftock hives ? we may reply, that it may be purchafed from other counties, in order to fupply ourfelves, as well as to feed our weak hives.

		HIVES.
In the 1. year, Sept. 1795, there would be		32,000
—— 2. —— —— 1796, ———————		64,000
—— 3. —— —— 1797, ———————		128,000
—— 4. —— —— 1798, ———————		256,000
—— 5. —— —— 1799, ———————		512,000
—— 6. —— —— 1800, ———————		1,024,000
—— 7. —— —— 1801, ———————		2,048,000

Thus, within the fhort period of feven years, the number of our bee-hives would be increaf-ed to no lefs than TWO MILLIONS and FORTY EIGHT THOUSAND HIVES. But allowing the forty eight thoufand to be difcounted for dead hives, there would ftill remain two millions of ftock hives. Although this number may appear to be large, yet there is no reafon to fuppofe, that the calculation is neither impoffible or improbable. But, even dropping the one half of this number, upon the fuppofition of loffes by bad feafons, &c. there would ftill remain, at the loweft eftimate, a clear MILLION of ftock hives; which, next year might produce FOUR MILLIONS of PINTS of HONEY, and ONE MILLION of POUNDS of WAX; and ftill keeps the ftock entire. With fuch a quantity, indeed, of thefe ufeful animals, and valuable commodities, we might reft contented; as fuch a quantity, befides every other advantage, would afford employment to hundreds of old

and

and poor people to watch them in fwarming time, and to make hives to receive the young colonies.

Another method, by which the number of our ftock hives may be more fpeedily increaf-ed in this country, might eafily be adopted. Should any one opulent proprietor, or a com-pany of individuals, incline to have 2000 or 3000 bee-hives, let a commiffion be fent by a proper perfon to Poland or Ruffia, where, in the month of Auguft efpecially, they could be pur-chafed at one third part of the price they gene-rally draw here : And I am perfuaded, if the Dantzick hives are made much in the fame form with ours, or in any other form that will admit of carriage, a fhip nearly loaded with other goods, which would help to pay her freight, might bring over a great number of them. Perhaps many will think this an extravagant attempt, but I am fo confident of its fuccefs, that if I were poffeffed of 1000 l. Sterling in ready cafh, I would fet fail for Dantzick, and rifk 800 l. of it upon the adven-ture. On bringing home my cargo of living bees, I would fpread them all over the king-dom : But, before fetting out upon fuch a voy-age, I would firft inform myfelf properly about

G   the

the form of the Dantzick hives, as well as about their prices, and whether they are to be got near the fea-coaſt ; as land carriage of bees is equally troubleſome, expenſive, and dangerous : But I would not be afraid to riſk 1000 bee-hives on board a ſhip ; for, I would rather carry them 4000 miles on ſhip-board, when properly packed, than 100 by land.

C H A P. VII.

ACCOUNT OF THE QUEEN BEE.

THE QUEEN, or MOTHER BEE, is eaſily diſtinguiſhed from all the other bees in the hive, by the form, ſize, and colour of her body. She is conſiderably longer, and her wings are much ſhorter in proportion to her body, than thoſe of the other bees. The wings of both common bees and drones, cover their whole bodies, whereas thoſe of the Queen ſcarce reach beyond the middle, ending about the third ring of her belly. Her hinder part is

far

far more tapering than thofe of the other bees:
Her belly and legs are yellower, and her upper
parts of a much darker colour than theirs.
She is alfo furnifhed with a fting, though fome
authors affert that fhe has none, having been
induced to form this opinion, becaufe fhe is
extremely pacific; fo much fo, indeed, that
one may handle her, and even teaze her as
much as he pleafes, without provoking her
refentment. For my part, I never could excite a Queen Bee to draw her fting, nor could
I even get a fight of it, but when I preffed her
body. The omnifcient Governor of Nature
has wifely ordained this majeftic infect to be
of a pacific difpofition; for, were fhe otherwife,—were fhe, like the other bees, of fo irritable a temper as to draw her fting on every
occafion, and to leave it in the body of her an-
tagonift, it would prove of dangerous and often fatal confequences to the whole hive; for
every bee, after lofing her fting, dies within a
day or two at the utmoft.

The Queen bee is folemn and calm in her de-
portment. A young Queen is a great deal fmaller in fize than a full grown one; being not
much longer than a common bee, and is therefore not fo eafily obferved when fought for.

When

When only three or four days old, fhe is very quick in her motions, and runs very fáft; but when pregnant with eggs, fhe becomes very large, and her body is heavy. When travelling, fhe drags along in a very flow manner, and is not very expeditious in flying. It is proper that every proprietor of bees fhould know the Queen, as it may often be of great advantage to him. The fureft way to know her is to get a fight of one from fome acquaintance, who keeps hives : or, if this cannot be obtained, he may fearch for her, by the above defcription, among fome fmall hives.

That this majeftic animal is a female, the very defignation fhe bears, of QUEEN, feems to imply that all modern authors are convinced, though many of the ancients were of a different opinion. But as it is alfo now unanimoufly admitted, that fhe lays every egg in the hive, fhe ought rather to be called the MOTHER BEE. For, indeed, from the beft obfervation that ever I could make, fhe poffeffes and exerts NO So-VEREIGNTY over the other bees. She evidences the greateft anxiety for the good of the commonwealth, with which fhe is connected; and, indeed, every member of it fhows an equal regard for her welfare. But I never could ob-

ferve,

ferve, that fhe iffues any pofitive orders, to be punctually obeyed by the other bees. The truth feems to be, that fhe and the other bees are all equally acquainted with their duty by *inftinct*, and have an equal pleafure in performing it, without waiting for orders from each other. That there is, neverthelefs, the greateft order and regularity among them, is certain; for they lay their plans and execute them in the beft poffible manner, by the influence of the above powerful fubftitute for reafon.

Almoft all writers, as formerly hinted, are of opinion, that the Queen lays three different kinds of eggs; viz. one kind for the production of a Queen Bee; another fpecies for that of the working bees, and a third for producing the Drones. It was alfo long a received opinion, that no Queen could lay eggs, that were capable of producing bees, without the affiftance of Drones. SCHIRACH †, on this fubject, refutes this doctrine, and entirely denies fuch an ufe of the Drones. He advances this opinion, that " the Queen lays eggs, which produce young " bees, without any communication with the Drones ;

† Paftor of KLEIN BAUTZEN, in UPPER LUSATIA, and Secretary to a Society of Naturalifts there.

" Drones ; and affirms that all the working
" bees are females in difguife ; every one of
" whom, in an early ftage of her exiftence, was
" capable of becoming a Queen ; from a know-
" ledge of which fact, fwarms may artificially
" be obtained from the early months of fpring,
" and in any fucceeding month, even to No-
" vember."

His experiments have been very numerous,
and obviate every doubt and objection.   He
performed the operation, upon one and the
fame ftock, for at leaft fifty or fixty times, from
mere fragments of the combs, &c. &c.   This
novel and wonderful doctrine excited no fmall
contention, and not a few counter experiments
among naturalifts on the Continent, without
being decided even by the great BONNET.   He
afferts, which is indeed the grand and decifive
proof, that " the practice of this art, (of rai-
" fing artificial Queens,) has already extended
" itfelf through Upper Lufatia, the Palatinate,
" Bohemia, Bavaria, Silefia, and feveral parts of
" Germany, and even of Poland."

That a Queen can be raifed from an egg in
a common cell, or, in other words, that the
felf-fame egg is capable of being reared up to
be either a Queen, or a common bee, as the

bees

bees pleafe, appears to me, from my own experiments, to be paft a doubt; and that a
Queen, who never faw a drone, can lay eggs,
which will produce bees, is equally certain.
Both of thefe facts will, I flatter myfelf, appear
to the curious and learned reader, to be clearly afcertained by the following experiments.

Long before I heard of Mr Schirach's theory, or experiments, I had often taken off
fwarms, without leaving any Queens or royal
cells in the mother hive; notwithftanding
which, they bred young Queens, which furprized me greatly how they had obtained them,
as the received opinion then was, that they
could not breed a Queen bee, if the old Queen
was taken away, before a royal cell was erected. But after feeing Schirach's fentiments on
this fubject, I thought his theory extremely
probable, according to what I had obferved a-
mong my own bees; and refolving to afcertain
the truth of it, I made many experiments of
my own, which all fucceeded to my wifhes.
But, in order to put the matter beyond all
doubt, I fhall relate an experiment I made with
a hive in fpring 1788, two months before the
ufual time of fwarming, and which clearly
afcertains both the facts at once. The hive
was

was beginning to carry well, and to breed faft, but it was not half full of bees. It had only one Queen, but neither Drone nor royal cell; neither of which could be expected at that feafon of the year, as it was about the middle of April. I took out the Queen, and moft part of the bees, and left the hive with only fome common bees, to hatch out the young brood in the cells, and provide themfelves with a Queen, but without leaving one fingle Drone. They did not difappoint me; for as foon as the melancholy intelligence pervaded the hive, that their loving mother was torn from them, they made a mourning kind of noife for their great lofs, for about two hours : After which, a general council, as it would feem, being called, the moft experienced fages, in the diftreffed republic, may be fuppofed to have advifed their brethren, " That it was in vain to mourn longer for the lofs of their mother and brothers; that although they were gone, and although they had at prefent no royal cell to raife another mother, yet they had ftill fufficient refources from nature and their own induftry; that they had power and means to raife a young monarch to the throne; that they had plenty of new laid eggs, and there-

fore

fore no time was to be loft, to raife a Queen
bee from one of them; otherwife the eggs
would all foon produce common bees, and
then all hopes of future progeny would ceafe
for ever, and their republic utterly perifh, for
want of a prolific mother to preferve and per-
petuate the race."

That the bees feemed to have had fome
fuch reafoning among them, appeared pretty
evident from their conduct; for about two
hours after the capture of the Queen, they all
fell bufily to work, and exerted themfelves a-
mazingly for two days; fome being employed in forming the royal cell, and others in in-
jecting into it a large quantity of thick whitifh liquid ftuff, pretty much refembling cream.
At the end of the 3d day, the royal cell was
completely formed; and, in the mean time,
the common cells were fealed up by the other
bees, who all continued bufily employed.
On the fifth day, the royal cell was confiderably enlarged, and I obferved as much of the a-
forefaid white ftuff in it, as would have half filled a thimble almoft, with a white maggot lying
on the top of it. On the feventh day, the bees
fealed it up, and, on the feventeenth day, the
young Queen came forth out of her little pa-

H   lace

lace, in all her pomp and majesty. On the twenty-fourth day, the young Queen became a MOTHER, and laid eggs; on the thirty-first day, these eggs were sealed up, and, on the for-ty-third day, a number of young bees emerged from the cells. About the same time I repeat-ed this experiment with other two hives, which both succeeded equally well.

I made another experiment with a different hive, out of which I took the Queen and most part of the bees. This hive had neither a roy-al cell nor drones in it, yet, in seventeen days thereafter, a Queen was reared, and on the 25th day she laid eggs. I then took out the young Queen again, leaving some new laid eggs in the old hive. Within eight days after, there was another royal cell erected and sealed up. This I immediately took out of the hive; but, upon inspecting the hive eight days there-after, I found neither Queen, eggs, nor royal cell, none of which indeed I expected. Upon taking a piece of comb, however, with eggs in it, out of another hive, and putting it into this hive, the bees erected another royal cell, which in due time produced another young Queen.

The advocates for the doctrine of the drones being males, and their aid being necessary for the

the propagation of bees, may perhaps plead, that although there were no drones in the hive, when I took the Queen from it, yet there might have been eggs laid in drone cells, which would come forward to be drones as foon as the young Queen, and fo impregnate her, and render her fit for breeding. But the contrary is the fact : for, when the old Queen was taken out of the hive, there was not a fingle egg in any of the drone cells. If there had, I would have feen the bees fitting upon the cells of the drone combs, as they did on thofe of the common bees, and on the royal cell. Befides, I turned up the hive every fecond day, during the whole period of forty-three days, in order to determine how long the bees took to erect the royal cell, and feal it up ; how many days elapfed before an egg produced a Queen ; how old the Queen was, before fhe began to lay eggs ; how many days paffed, before thefe eggs produced common bees ; and, above all, whether the Queen needed the agency of the drones, to enable her to become a mother. To arrive at a certainty on this point, I often turned the bees over in the hive with a fmall ftick, in fearch of young drones in drone cells, but could not difcover the fmalleft vef-

H 2   tige

tige of them. But the young Queen, on the
10th day of her age, began to lay eggs in
drone cells, which produced young drones in
the hive about fixteen days thereafter. Having repeated this laft experiment again and a-
gain, I can now affirm, with the utmoft confidence and certainty, that the common, or
working bees, are endowed with the powerful
faculty of raifing a Queen bee, from an egg,
in a common cell, when their community
ftands in need of one.

Their method is this: They make choice
of a common cell with an egg in it, and inject fome white liquid matter, from their probofcis, of a thickifh fubftance. They then
begin to build upon the edges of the cell, and
enlarge it. On the third day, it appears fairly
on the outfide of the comb, in the form of a
royal cell, and may now be properly fo denominated. On the fifth day, the cell being now
greatly enlarged, and a great deal of the whitifh matter thrown into it, the royal maggot
appears in the form of a femicircle, not unlike
a new moon, being biggeft in the middle part,
and fmall at each end. In this form it is to
be feen for two days, fwimming on the top,

and

and in the midft of the faid matter in the cell ;
and on the feventh day it is fealed up.

During this period, our young princefs undergoes various metamorphofes. I have opened the royal cell on the tenth day, and have
found the maggot ftill on the top of the white
liquor ; and having taken it into my hand to
fhow it to any friend, it would have moved for
a fhort time, although at this period, it had not
the fmalleft refemblance to a bee, being ftill only a maggot. But on the fourteenth or fifteenth
day, the metamorphofis is fo complete, that inftead of a grofs white worm, forth comes a
charming young Queen bee, † arrayed in all
her glory. From the whole of thefe experiments, therefore, which I have repeated on various occafions, I can pofitively affirm, that the
Queen bee is capable of becoming a mother,
without fo much as feeing a drone ; and that
the

† The fame procefs, or nearly fo, is ufed by the common bees,
to bring forward both their own fpecies and drones, by throw-
ing the whitifh matter on the eggs, and fealing them up, till the
maggots undergo the ufual changes in the cells, &c. And each
egg generally produces a bee in about fourteen or fixteen days.
I have feen them differ two or three days in point of time. Perhaps an egg, fhould the bees let it alone and injeſt no matter upon it, might, neverthelefs, keep warm for 8 days, and produce a
bee at laſt.

the doctrines of almoft all former writers on this
fubject, (Schirach and one or two more except-
ed,) who affirm that the Queen cannot breed
without the agency of the drones, or males,
as they call them, is founded on a miftake.
For a fmall piece of comb, with common eggs
in it, may be taken and put into a box along
with 400 common bees, and tranfported 1000
miles from a Drone ; and yet the bees will rear
a Queen from one of thofe eggs, and that young
Queen will lay eggs, which in due time will
produce Queens, Commons and Drones. But
whether every egg in the common cells of the
hive can be nourifhed up to produce a Queen,
I dare not pofitively fay ; although I am much
inclined to think fo, as I can fafely affirm, that
not above one in a dozen of my experiments, in
rearing Queens from what are called *common
eggs*, (i. e. eggs that commonly produce working
bees,) has ever yet failed, when I either made
the trial by way of experiment, or adopted the
plan as a matter of œconomy. Sometimes a
fingle egg has failed in making the experiment ;
but this might have happened from fome other
accidental caufe. As a proof of this, I offer to
rear 20 Queens, if not 30, out of one hive, during the courfe of one fummer. For I have,
within

within thefe laft fix years, caufed the bees to rear, from eggs taken from common cells, which the bees would otherwife have reared up for working bees, no fewer than 200 *artificial* Queens ; and which Queens laid eggs, that came forward to be bees, in the fame manner as other Queens, which may, for diftinction's fake, be ftiled *natural* ones.

Sometimes, when I have taken the Queen out of a hive, and left none but common bees in it, after looking for the fpace of fourteen or fixteen days, for royal cells, as ufual in fuch cafes, I have obferved, that, inftead of Queens being produced, there were three or four royal cells, which contained nothing in them, except that fome of them had a red tough matter, of a hard kind of fubftance, about the fize of a pea, which would tear, but would not break : while others of them would have contained neither egg, maggot, nor chryfalis, but were quite empty. Thefe empty cells I fhall, for diftinction's fake, call *falfe royal cells.* What was the intention of the bees, in rearing thefe falfe royal cells, I cannot determine. The bees were furely fenfible, that there were no young bees in them : and yet they would have allowed them

to

to continue in the hive for many months.
One circumftance inclines me to think, that
the bees intended them to be of fome ufe for
rearing Queens, as I never faw thefe falfe royal cells reared, but when the hive wanted a
Queen. I am equally certain, however, on the
other hand, that I have never once feen an egg
or decayed maggot in any of them. I own
that fome common cells will fometimes be fealed up, as if there were young bees in them, although none would ever appear. All of thefe,
however, had eggs in them at firft, which had
decayed and rotten, by cold or fome other accident. But this I never found to be the cafe,
in thofe falfe royal cells, not one of which appeared to have ever had one in them. Therefore, when we leave a hive without a Queen,
we cannot pofitively fay, that the bees will
rear one for themfelves : yet were the practice
eligible in every other refpect, we might truft
to it, as fcarcely one cafe in a dozen fails. But
if a royal cell, on the 2d, 3d, or 4th day, after it is erected, appear to have an egg, or
fome of the whitifh matter in it, a Queen may
be depended upon, to be produced in due time,
if no accident prevent.

That

That the Queen and the common or working bees are of the fame fex in the egg, and yet that they can rear up bees of every fpecies between them, appears to me to be no more wonderful than true *. Whether the additional matter thrown into the enlarged cell, along with the egg, is of a generative or nutritive nature, I cannot yet pofitively determine, altho' I rather incline to think it is of the former kind.—But there are confiderable difficulties on both fides. For, if we fay the white matter is of a generative quality, then we muft fuppofe that the working bees are males; although it muft appear very unaccountable, that the *fame egg* fhould be capable of rearing either a *male* or a *female*, at the option of the working bees:—which, however, upon this fuppofition,

I   appears

---

* Whether the bees can rear up one of thofe eggs that are laid in drone cells, to beccme a Queen or a common bee; or whether they can rear eggs that have been laid in common cells, to become drones, is not yet afcertained. This queftion, however, might eafily be decided, by putting a piece of comb with drone eggs in it, along with 400 common bees; and, by repeating the experiment 6 or 8 times, it might foon be difcovered, whether the bees could raife one of thofe drone eggs to be a Queen bee. I rather incline to think, that the eggs laid in drone cells cannot be raifed to be any other but drone bees, and that thofe laid in common cells can never be reared to become drones.

appears clearly proved, by Schirach's experiments and my own. On the other hand, if we hold it to be of a nutritive nature, then we suppose the Queen to be a hermaphrodite, or *self-prolific*, without the assistance of any other creature. It is indeed reported, that the whole genus of snails are hermaphrodites, and that each individual of the species is endued with both sexes.

But although I have not a doubt as to the fact, that an egg in a common cell is capable of being nourished up to produce a Queen, yet I rather doubt, whether any great improvement can be made of this discovery, so as to increase the quantity of honey and wax; as it is not a great number of hives that will produce that effect, but only real good ones. I also doubt, whether more hives can be reared by this method, as our bees generally produce more Queens naturally, than they are able to supply with a sufficient number of common bees to compose a proper swarm with; as appears from their killing the supernumerary ones, which they have no need of.—Often, for instance, in a garden containing four stock hives in May, they will breed perhaps 24 Queens during the summer, but will kill two thirds of them, and send off

the

the other 8, with as many young fwarms.—It muft be allowed, however, that hives will fome-times ly long out; and, therefore, if the owner had a fpare Queen, he might eafily rear new fwarms with them, which he cannot fafely do without them.

C H A P. VIII.

ACCOUNT OF THE DRONE BEE.

Tнe drones are a fpecies of bees, well known to every Bee-mafter, and may eafily be diftinguifhed from the common or working bees. They are both larger and longer in the body. Their heads are round, their eyes full, and their tongues fhort. The form of the belly differs from thofe of both Queen and common bees; and their colour is darker than either. They have no fting, and they make a much greater noife when flying, than either the Queen or the common bees;—a peculiarity of itfelf fufficient to diftinguifh them.

I 2   The

The drones are, by almoſt all writers reckoned the males, (See p. 62,) and are ſo ſtiled by
moſt authors ; but for my part I neither know
what to call them, nor of what uſe they are,
although I have often thought upon the ſubject, yet I cannot be ſatisfied with any theory
I ever heard of.   Various conjectures have
been made with reſpect to their uſe.   Although
almoſt all agree that they are the males, and
couple with the Queen ; yet they acknowledge
that they never ſaw an inſtance of any one of them
in the act with her.   It is ſurely wonderful, if
the drones are the males, that they ſhould have
eſcaped the prying eyes of philoſophers in all
ages, whereas, almoſt every eye has detected
ſmaller inſects in the act.

SWAMMERDAM, ſenſible of this, to ſhelter
himſelf, flies to that falſe refuge, that the *ſmell*
of the drones anſwers the ſame end as copula-
tion.   Others ſay, that their heat is neceſſary
for hatching the young bees.   But this argument has no weight with me ; as bee-hives
have moſt part of their bees bred, and are well
nigh ſwarming, before any number of drones
appear in the hive.   Beſides, by the time that
they become numerous, ſo as their heat might
do good in that reſpect, the heat is generally

ſo

fo great, that the bees have too much of it; and, therefore, often ly out in the fore part of their hive to get air. It is therefore plain, that they need not be at the expence of maintaining a parcel of idle gluttons, for the fake of increafing what would do them more harm than good.

That the Queen ftands in no need of their affiftance to fecundate or impregnate her, has already been obferved, and appears plain, from this confideration, that fhe lays eggs, which produce young bees, without having had any previous communication with the drones. I will not, however, fuppofe that the drones are of no ufe in the hive; but that the Queen lays eggs which produce young bees, without fo much as feeing a drone, I can with the utmoft confidence affirm.

The advocates for the old doctrine, that the drones are males, alledge, that they impregnate the Queen, before their brethren kill them. According to this theory, fhe fhould continue for no lefs a period than feven or eight months, with about 12,000 impregnated eggs in her ovarium, which would certainly make her appear very large during the whole of that period. But it is unneceffary to wafte

arguments

arguments in refutation of this doctrine, as I have already shown (pages 56, 57, 58) that I have repeatedly had Queens breed and lay eggs, and those eggs become bees, although these Queens were bred seven months after all the drones were dead, and some weeks before any new ones were hatched. These experiments, I think, are sufficient to silence all the arguments advanced by the advocates for the drone system. Mr DEBRAW, indeed, creates *little drones*, and gives them power to live all the year, and to impregnate the Queen at pleasure. But as room does not permit me to narrate the experiments whereby he attempts to prove this, I shall content myself with stating his sentiments in as few words as possible. He asserts, that, besides the common large drones, which every person, acquainted with bees, knows at first sight, there is a small kind of drones, which are, to all appearance, like the common bees, there being no visible difference, except that they have no sting, which he discovered by immersion in water, and pressure. After relating an experiment on this head, he says, " I once more " immersed all the bees" (of a small swarm) " in water, and when they appeared to be in " a senseless state, I gently pressed every one of " them

" them between my fingers, in order to diftin-
" guifh thofe armed with ftings from thofe
" that had none, which laft I might fufpect to
" be males. Of thefe I found fifty feven,
" exactly of the fize of common bees, yielding
" a little whitifh liquor on being preffed be-
" tween the fingers."

He farther alledges, that if there be only a
Queen and bees that have ftings in a hive, although the Queen lays eggs, yet if fhe has no
drones to inject the feminal matter upon them,
the eggs will ftill remain unproductive, and
will decay, even although there were 1000 bees
with ftings in the hive. In anfwer to this, I
fhall here narrate an experiment I made feveral years ago.

On the firft of Sept. 1788, I took all the
bees out of a hive that was breeding very faft,
and in which I found only four drones, which
I killed. I put the bees into a hive that had
nothing in it but empty combs. After waiting ten days, upon looking between the combs,
I found maggots newly fealed up, in the cells.
I then took out all the bees, and fhook them into a tub full of water, from which immerfion
I recovered them gradually, and while doing
this, I preffed each bee individually, to try if

I

I could difcover any of thofe ftinglefs little
drones ; but not one appeared, all of them
having ftings, to the number af 3000. After
this I fearched the old hive I had taken them
out of, and cut out all the combs that had eggs
or young in them ; among which I found fome
cells that had new laid eggs in them ; others
whofe eggs were converted into a fmall worm,
and others fome with maggots in them. I then
reftored the Queen, and all the bees, putting
them into the fame hive again, but without
leaving a fingle egg in it. During the fucceding
twenty days, I infpected the hive, and found the
bees, in fine weather, working with great alacrity, a fure fign that the Queen was breeding a-
gain. After this, on turning up the hive, and
cutting out one of the brood combs, I found
new laid eggs in fome of them ; others containing maggots ; befides fome young bees,
almoft ready to emerge from their cells.

I made another experiment, about the fame
time, upon a hive that had fome brood combs,
but had not had a large drone for feveral weeks
preceding. This hive did not contain above 500
bees, a circumftance that was in my favour, as,
being lefs numerous, the trouble was proportionally lefs. I carried the hive into a clofe
room

room in my houfe, that not a fingle bee might efcape me ; but, after repeating the former experiment of immerfing them in water, recovering, and preffing them one by one, I found that every one of them had a fting.

I think thefe experiments may fatisfy any unprejudiced perfon, that there is no fuch creature in exiftence as a fmall drone bee ; unlefs it be in Mr DEBRAW's *brain.* But, if Mr Debraw, who fays he can find fifty-feven in a fmall fwarm of bees, will fend me the odd feven, I will give him one of my beft hives for them, and I think he will not fay that they are ill fold.

I have often had good hives, with few or no drones in them, during the whole year. Mr KEYS is wrong, when he fays, a top fwarm will not thrive without drones, for I am certain of the contrary. In fummer 1785, I took off four fwarms of my own in one day, without a fingle drone in one of them ; yet they all throve well, and the bees bred drones in them about four weeks thereafter.

Although I cannot determine of what ufe the drones are to a hive, unlefs it be to help to confume the honey, which they are very well qualified to do, yet it is obfervable that the

K   beft

beſt hives produce them earlieſt in the year; as they generally appear in ſuch hives about the beginning of May, and the working bees put an end to their exiſtence at Lammas, at which period I generally aſſiſt them as much as I am able.

After my firſt work upon this ſubject appeared, I had the honour of a converſation with two very intelligent gentlemen in my neighbourhood, who declared their ſatisfaction with the arguments I had formerly advanced. I alſo repeated, in the preſence of one of them, ſome of the experiments I had made, to prove that the common bees are endued with the power of rearing any egg, from a common cell, to become a Queen, when the community ſtands in need of one; and that a Queen, although ſhe never ſaw a drone, will, at a proper age, lay eggs in abundance, which, again, by the aſſiſtance of the common bees, will produce Queens, commons, and drones, as well as thoſe eggs that are laid by Queens, who are ſurrounded with drones in the hives to which they belong.

After ſeeing theſe experiments, of which he expreſſed his approbation, I had another converſation with both theſe gentlemen, when
they

they afked me,—What then is the ufe of the
" drone ?"—In anfwer to this, I candidly acknowledged that I could not tell, as any conjecture, that I could form refpecting their ufe,
appeared to be attended with infurmountable
objections. We all agreed, however, that they
certainly muft be of fome ufe, as Nature, or,
more properly fpeaking, the GOD of Nature,
does nothing in vain.

One of the gentlemen faid, that, perhaps
bees might be like fome other infects, whofe
males were not neceffary in every act of generation; and that, perhaps, although a Queen
bee, who had never feen a drone, could lay an
egg which would produce a Queen, and that
Queen again do the fame, and thus the production of Queens and bees be continued with
equal fuccefs, for perhaps fix, eight, or ten generations; yet it might perhaps turn out, that
thefe Queens would gradually become more
and more unfruitful, and at laft grow altogether barren, unlefs they fhould cohabit with
the drones. The other gentleman, however,
was of opinion, that if one Queen was fruitful without the agency of the drones, every
other one would be fo likewife, to the end of
the world.

There

There is one thing, however, that feems to favour the former gentleman's conjecture; viz. that fome hives, which had not a fingle drone in them, have been known to breed well for one fummer, pretty well the next, and even tolerably the third; but at laft, have breed drones, and thereby turned out much more prolific thereafter: although it muft be owned, that fuch hives generally fail at laft. Seeing the drones are great confumers of honey, though they do nothing to provide any, fhould the above conjecture, therefore, turn out to be true, a practical inference may naturally be drawn, that a hive may thrive fully as well, or rather better, for 3 or 4 years, without drones than with them; after which period, they might again be introduced into the hive, for the purpofe of renewing the prolific powers of the Queen, and prevent the royal race from becoming barren or extinct. It may be farther obferved, as an additional argument in favour of the above conjecture, that although the Queen and her daughter, none of whom ever faw a drone, might lay abundance of eggs, which would all produce bees; yet they might probably have laid a great many more, had the drones been in the hive with them.

I

I muft confefs, it appears fomewhat para-
doxical, to fay that females will breed fuccefs-
fully for feveral generations without the affiftance of the males ; and yet at laft prove barren, and give over breeding altogether, till their
prolific powers are renewed by frefh males co-
habitating with them. But however paradox-
ical or unaccountable it may appear, that is
not a fufficient reafon for us to reprobate the
fuppofition ; as there are many of the arcana
of nature that are equally wonderful and unaccountable, and the elucidation of which has
hitherto baffled the inveftigation of the moft
penetrating geniufes, and deepeft enquirers into the fecrets of natural philofophy.

One of the above-mentioned gentlemen defired me to try an experiment, and endeavour
to afcertain the fact, whether the want of
drones will occafion a gradual barrenefs to take
place in a fucceffion of Queens. My anfwer
was, that I had long entertained an idea of a
plan, whereby I am perfuaded that I could dive
into, and probably difcover this fecret of Nature ; but that the execution would both require time, and be attended with a confiderable degree of expence, by the lofs of many
hives, which at prefent I do not find myfelf
inclined

inclined to rifk. Whereupon he defired me to make the experiment with his own hives, which I engaged to do the firft leifure opportunity: And as it may doubtlefs be a piece of ufeful natural philofophy, I fhall certainly communicate the refult of my inquiries to the public on a future occafion.

CHAP. IX.

ACCOUNT OF THE WORKING BEE.

THE WORKING, or COMMON BEES, are fo often feen by every body, and fo univerfally well known, that a particular defcription may almoft appear unneceffary, although, for uniformity's fake, I fhall give it. They are fmaller in fize than either the Queen or the drone bees; and, the denomination they have fo juftly obtained, of *Working* Bees, plainly denotes their fuperior induftry, in labouring for the whole hive.

The

The common bee as well as the other two
fpecies of that valuable infect, confifts of three
parts, viz. the head, which is attached by
a narrow kind of neck, to the reft of the
body ;—the breaft, or middle part ;—and the
belly, which is nearly feparated from the breaft
by an infection or divifion, and connected with
it by another narrow neck or junction. There
are two eyes in the head, of an oblong figure,
black, tranfparent, and immovable. The
mouth or jaws, like thofe of fome fpecies of
fifh, open to the right and left, and ferve inftead of hands, to carry out of the hive whatever encumbers or offends them. In the mouth
there is a long probofcis, or trunk, with which
the bees fuck up the fweets from the flowers.
They have four wings faftened to their middle part, by which they are not only enabled to fly with heavy loads, but alfo to
make thofe well known founds and hummings,
to each other, that are fuppofed to be their only form of fpeech. They have alfo fix legs
faftened to their middle. The two foremoft
of thefe are the fhorteft, and with thefe they
unload themfelves of their treafures. The two
in the middle are fomewhat longer ; and the
two laft are the longeft of all. On the outfide

o .

of the middle joint of thefe laft, there is a fmall cavity in the form of a marrow fpoon, in which the bees collect, by degrees, thofe loads of wax they carry home to their hives. This hollow grove is peculiar to the working bee. Neither the Queen nor the drones have any refemblance of it.

The belly is ornamented or diftinguifhed with fix rings; and contains, befides the inteftines of the animal, the honey bladder, the venom bladder, and the fting. The honey bladder is a refervoir, into which is depofited the honey that the bee fips from the cups of the flowers, after it has paffed through the probofcis, and through the narrow pipes, that connect the head, breaft and belly of the bee. This bladder, when full, is of the fize of a fmall pea, and is fo tranfparent, that the colour of the honey can be diftinguifhed through it. The fting is fituated at the extremity of the belly, and the head or root of it is placed contiguous to the fmall bladder that contains the venom. It is connected to the belly by certain fmall mufcles, by means of which the bee can dart it out, and draw it in, with great force and quicknefs. In length it is about the 6th part of an inch. It is of a horny fubftance;

is

is biggeft at the root, and tapers gradually towards the point, which is extremely fmall and fharp ; and when examined by the microfcope, appears to be polifhed exceedingly fmooth.*. It is hollow within, like a tube, that the venomous liquor may pafs through it, when it ftrikes any animal, which it does the very inftant that the fting pierces the fkin, and infinuates itfelf into the wound ; which proves mortal to many fmall animals, as well as to the bee herfelf, when fhe leaves her fting in the wound ; as it draws after it the bladder, and fometimes part of the entrails of the bee.

Thefe working bees may be faid to compofe the whole community, except in the feafon of the drones, which hardly lafts three months. During all the other nine months, there are no other bees in the hive, except them and the Queen. The whole labour of the hive is performed by them. They build the combs, collect the honey, bring it home, and ftore it up in their waxen magazines. They rear up the eggs, to produce young Queens, common bees and drones ; they carry out all incumbrances that are in the hives ; they defend the community againft enemies of every kind, and kill all the drones.

L   CHAP.

C H A P. X.

DIRECTIONS TO GUARD AGAINST THE STING OF A BEE, WITH THE METHOD OF CURE.

As we muſt now proceed to the handling of our induſtrious inſects, it is neceſſary to put our readers on their guard againſt their ſtings.

Unleſs they are hurt, provoked, or affronted, bees ſeldom make uſe of their ſtings ; but they are ſo extremely irritable, that whoever wiſhes to be on a friendly footing with them muſt beware of giving them the ſmalleſt offence. They will hazard their lives, rather than let an affront paſs unrevenged ; and, when exaſperated near their hives, one may as well take a lion by the beard, or a bear by the ſnout, and expect to come off unpuniſhed, as to hope to capitulate with them.

When a perſon has any thing to do about his bees, which, he thinks, may provoke their vengeance, and which, nevertheleſs, muſt be done, ſuch as making them ſwarm, uniting light hives, &c. then he muſt equip himſelf

properly

properly, by putting on his harnefs, * and keeping it on, as long as their rage continues. But
when they are furprifed or frightened by rapping on the hive, they will be very pacific,
and will not attempt to fting. After which,
the Bee-mafter may fafely throw off his harnefs, and even his coat, by which he will be
more fit for performing bufinefs with them.

But fhould they be greatly enraged, the
beft method, if there is a houfe or open door
near, is to run as quickly as poffible into it,
and fhut them out, (for it is eafy to out-run
them,) and thus prevent them from following.
In fuch a cafe they will fly about the door for
fome time in great rage, impatient for an opening

L 2   to

---

* The HARNESS, or SAFEGUARD, fhould be formed on this plan.
Let a net be knit with fuch fmall mefhes, that a bee cannot pafs
through. Silk, gauze, catgut, crape, or any thing woven of a
fine thread, will anfwer equally well. The fafeguard muft be
made large enough to cover a man's hat, head, and neck, and to
tie clofe together before his breaft with a ftring. In tying it,
great caution fhould be obferved, that not the fmalleft chink or
opening be left for a bee to get in at; otherwife the remedy
will prove worfe than the difeafe; as thofe that get in would fting
with the utmoft virulence, and it would be impoffible to get either the ftings or the bees quickly out from under the harnefs.
The hands fhould be covered with a pair of gloves, and the legs
with a pair of coarfe ftockings, or two pairs of fine ones, as the
bees will often fting the legs through one pair.

to get in ; but the perfon muft take care to remain clofe prifoner, till his winged enemies retire. But if there be no houfe of refuge at
hand, where he can retire by rapid flight, he
fhould by no means retire gradually, but rather ftand ftill like a ftatue, or ly down flat upon
the ground, without any motion, with his face
downwards, in which cafe he may get off with
only two or three ftings ; but if he attempts to
fly and the bees overtake him, they will fting
him in fo many parts at once, that he may
not come off with lefs than one or two dozen
of wounds.

After their fury is abated, and the remem-
brance of the affront entirely obliterated, the
bee-mafter may then renew his acquaintance with his winged labourers ; and if he
comes in a humble manner, and walks gently and fubmiffively among them, they will
treat him kindly. In every bufinefs one has
to do with bees, he muft do it in a calm,
foft, gentle, and fubmiffive way ; he muft
take care not to approach them in a rafh, hafty
manner, puffing and blowing, or accompanied
with any thing that has a difagreeable or un-
favoury fmell, as their organs of fmelling appear to be very acute. In a word, gentle reader,

er, you muſt approach your bees, as you would
appear before your patron, when you are going
to aſk a favour of him ; and not, as you would
meet an opponent in a duel, unleſs you be
armed cap-a-pce.

When the bees attack a perſon who is walking among them, let him put them gently a-
ſide from his face with his hand, or thruſt
his head into a buſh, and they will ſoon leave
him.

When they are offended at any perſon, the
chief parts they aim at are the face and hands,
knowing theſe parts are moſt vulnerable. But
if the face and hands are covered, they will
ſurround him, and try to diſcover any aperture in his ſhirt, neck, breaſt, ſleeves, breeches-
knees, &c. and if they find an opening at
the ſmalleſt ſlit or crevice, they will puſh in at
it, and leave their ſtings, with their venom behind, though they loſe their lives in the conflict.

The hair of the head, beard, and eye-brows,
are all very offenſive to bees, and if they accidentally light on any of them, they will ſting
that very inſtant. When at work in the field,
they never offer to ſting, let them be ever ſo
much affronted. One may then chaſe them
from

from flower to flower, without provoking them to sting : they rather, on such occasions, fly off from the intruder, as unworthy of their notice.

The stings of bees have very different effects on different persons. There are some persons, upon whom the sting of a bee produces neither inflammation nor pain. Such people need use no precaution, even when they are sure to receive many stings. Upon others, again, the sting of a bee, ·occasions such exquisite pain, accompanied with swelling and inflammation, that nothing can terrify them more than the sight of a bee. This last class should not be discouraged. I myself have felt very different effects from their stings at different times. The seldomer I am stung, and the longer interval that occurs since I was last wounded, the greater pain I feel, and the more I swell : but when I am stung twice or thrice in a day, I value it not a pin. I have sometimes received forty stings in a day without swelling in the least. The reason of this I presume not to account for ; I only mention the fact, leaving it to medical people, or those who have studied the nature of animal poisons, to investigate the cause.

Many

Many remedies have been prefcribed, moft of them to little purpofe, to cure the wound received by a fting. Oil of olives, or any mild oil, is thought by many to be effectual. Bruifed parfley is recommended by others; the honey taken out of the bee that inflicted the wound, is prefcribed by a third clafs. Some fay, that the fweet fpirit of vitriol, well rubbed into the wound, will prevent both the pain and the fwelling. Repeated experiments, however, have fhown that the eafe, received from any of the above medicines, is not always to be depended upon, and therefore may be imputed as much to accidental circumftances, fuch as the wounded perfon's ftate of health, blood, &c. as to any peculiar fpecific virtue; although I doubt not, but that any or all of them may fometimes afford relief.

The fting and its poifon are injected in a moment, and the pain and fwelling inftantly fucceed, when fuch remedies are often very diftant. My remedies are more fimple, and one or other of them is always at hand. The moment I am wounded, after pulling out the fting, I take a blade of kail, dock, afh, or almoft any green leaf of any plant or fhrub neareft me, and, bruifing it a little, rub the
juice

juice into the wound. When near water, I wash the wound, or apply a wet cloth, which I have sometimes found give relief. But, indeed, I do not, once in a dozen of instances, apply any remedy at all, except pulling out the sting, as it seldom makes me uneasy; and I know a short time and a little patience will afford an infallible cure.

C H A P. XI.

How to choose stock hives in September.

Any person, who intends to erect an apiary, must take particular care to have it filled with proper inhabitants. He must be peculiarly attentive to this, as all his future profit and pleasure, or loss and vexation, will, in general, depend upon it. He must therefore pay the utmost attention to the choice of his stock hives; for the man who takes care to keep good stock hives will soon gain considerably by them; but he who keeps bad ones, will, be-

fides

fides a great deal of trouble, and little or no fuccefs, foon become a broken Bee-mafter.

In September every ftock hive ought to contain as much honey, as will fupply the bees with food, till June following; and as many bees as will preferve heat in the hive, and thereby refift the feverity of a cold winter, and act as fo many valiant foldiers, to defend the community from the invafions of foreign enemies in fpring. And, as September may be faid to be the bee-mafter's feed time, as well as his harveft, we fhall begin with it, and go round the circle of the year, giving fuch directions as are neceffary to be obferved in the different feafons, till we arrive again at the fame period. Therefore the bee-mafter fhould purchafe a proper number of hives in Auguft, or September, when they are at the cheapeft rate. They fhould be full of combs, and well ftored with bees and honey; and fhould weigh at leaft 30lb. each; if heavier, fo much the better; for light hives run a great rifk of perifhing by famine, unlefs the bees are fupplied with food; which will coft as much expence, and a great deal more trouble, * befides a con-

M   fiderable

* However, when a fufficient number of good fingle hives
for

siderable rifk of their dying at laft, after all this extraordinary trouble and expence. Whereas, a well chofen hive of 30lb. weight, allowing 12lb. for the empty hive, bees, combs, &c. will contain 18lb. of honey, which will fupply the bees with food till next June ; a time, when, it may be prefumed, they will find abundance of provifions for themfelves among the flowers.

When a choice can be obtained, the youngeft hives fhould always be preferred, becaufe old hives are liable to vermin, and other accidents. But although a hive fhould be four or five years old, it fhould not be rejected, if it poffeffes thefe two effential qualities, plenty of bees, and abundance of honey ; but, if

either

for ftock cannot be obtained, they may be made up, by conjoining the bees and honey of two or three light hives into one, and thereby making one tolerably good hive out of feveral bad ones. The method of doing this fhall be noticed afterwards ; but it is a meafure that ought never to be adopted but in cafes of neceffity. For neither fuch conjunctions of light hives, nor feeding of bees ought to be adopted, at this feafon, on purpofe to make them ftand the winter's cold, if they can poffibly be avoided. Indeed, fometimes very light hives, with few bees in them, will ftand through the courfe of a mild winter, and do well the following fummer ; but fuch hives are at beft precarious, and therefore not to be depended upon.

either of thefe be a-wanting, the purchafer
will regret his bad bargain when it is too late.

C H A P. XII.

OF THE REMOVING OF BEE-HIVES.

In the removal of hives, the diſtance, to
which they are to be removed, muſt be chiefly conſidered. If it is ſmall, they may be
tranſported in a hand barrow, carried by two
men ;—or they may be carried on a man's or
woman's head, in the manner that a milk-maid
carries her pails.

To prevent the bees from coming out during the carriage, a little ſtraw or graſs may
be put into the mouth of the hives. But, in
warm weather, the greateſt care muſt be taken, not to ſuffocate them with too much
heat ; eſpecially if there is a great number of
bees in the hive. For this purpoſe, they muſt
not be ſo cloſely ſhut up, as not to admit abun-

M 2   dance

dance of frefh air. For, the great heat of the bees, when no air is admitted, will melt the combs and the honey, and fuffocate or drown the bees. In this manner, valuable hives have often been loft in the fummer feafon, by ignorant perfons, who had been employed to tranfport them, fhutting up the door of the hive fo clofe, that no air could get in. The proper method to prevent the bees from coming out of the hive, in cafe of removal, in warm weather, or indeed at any time, and at the fame time to admit a circulation of air, is, to get a piece of lead or tin plate, pierced full of fmall holes, and fixed to the entry of the hive. This will anfwer both purpofes, by admitting frefh air, and at the fame time preventing the bees from flying away.

When the diftance is great, and there is a confiderable number of hives to be tranfported, (perhaps to the diftance of 6, 12, 20 or 50, miles) into an in-land country, carriages that move on fprings are by all means to be preferred. When thefe cannot be obtained, the hives may eafily be carried on carts or waggons, in cold weather, by placing them with their bottoms upmoft on large quantities of ftraw, hay, or any other foft article. By this method I have

carried

carried 20 hives at one time, with very little damage, either to the bees or the combs. Great care muſt be taken in placing them in the cart or waggon, that one hive may not interrupt or intercept the current of air from another. In hot ſultry weather, the removal ſhould be made in the night.

Before placing the hives in the carriages, every one of them ſhould be lifted off the ſtool it uſually ſtands on, and placed upon a piece of cloth about three feet ſquare. This cloth ſhould be of the ſame texture, with thoſe kinds of which window blinds, or cheeſe-cloths are made, that it may admit air, at the ſame time, that it effectually prevents the bees from eſcaping out of the hives. Let it be drawn cloſe up, around the edges of the hive, and, when properly ſecured to it with pack-thread, not a ſingle bee will get out. All this ſhould be done the evening before they are removed.

The utmoſt care ſhould alſo be taken, that no other opening be left at any other part of the hive, for the bees to get out at, as the moſt dangerous conſequences might ariſe, as the jolting of the vehicle might provoke the bees to ſting both the driver and the horſes; which might occaſion the overturning of the carriage, and

and of courfe not only rifk the deftruction of the whole cargo, with the carriage and horfes, but even the life of the driver himfelf.

Another method, if the diftance is great, I would recommend as preferable to every other, where it can be obtained, viz. carriage on fhip-board, either by fea, canals, lakes, or navigable rivers. By this mode of conveyance, the bees run no rifk of being jolted or hurt in the leaft, provided they are properly ftowed in the veffel. This laft winter, (1794,—5,) I carried twenty hives on fhip-board, with great fafety, to a gentleman about 300 miles diftant. I would, therefore, earneftly recommend water carriage wherever it is practicable, as preferable to every other mode of conveyance whatever; for I would rather carry a number of bee-hives 4000 miles by fea, than 100 miles by land carriage.

CHAP

C H A P. XIII.

HOW TO PREPARE STOCK HIVES FOR WINTER.

AFTER the hives are brought home, if room will permit, let every hive be placed two or three yards afunder, that the bees of one hive may not interfere with thofe of another, as is fometimes the cafe, when the hives are feated near one another, or upon the fame ftandard; for the bees, miftaking their own hives, alight fometimes at the wrong door, and a battle en-fues, wherein one or more may lofe their lives. There fhould not be too many hives in one place. Eight or nine are fufficient for one garden*; and as many more may be placed

at

* When too many hives are placed in one apiary, they are often troublefome in fwarming time. by the fwarms going to-gether, and by robbing one another, which they often do in Spring and Autumn, as will be fhown afterwards. Befides, when one has to feed them, the fmell of the honey entices them to fteal from each other, which fometimes occafions many bat-tles, whereby many of the bees are killed. But when there are

not

at about half a mile's diftance in every direction ; and thus the whole kingdom, or even the
whole ifland, might be covered with bee-hives,
at proper regular diftances, wherever there is
a fufficiency of food for the bees to work on.

The hives fhould be placed on boards or ftools,
made of well feafoned wood. Thefe boards fhould
be made a little broader than the bottom of the
hives, and fhould projeƈt about fix inches before the entry to it, that the bees may have a
fufficient breadth to alight upon, when they return from the fields.   When a proper place is
fixed on, where the hive is to be ereƈted, let
three ftakes be driven into the ground, till the
tops of them are within ten inches of it, and the
foremoft ftake one inch lower than the other
two.   The ftool with the hive on it may then
be placed upon thefe ; and at fun-fet, let the
fkirts of the hive be plaftered all clofe to the
board with plafter lime.   Next, let two fmall
holes be cut, in the under fide of a fmall piece
of hard wood, which muft be fixed to the entry
of the hive with lime.   Thefe holes muft juft
                                                      be

not too many hives in one place, they are not under fo much temp-
tation to enter into fuch confliƈts.   But at the fame time, twenty or thirty may be placed in one large apiary, and all do very
well, although the other method is rather to be preferred.

be wide enough to admit the largeſt bee, but
no wider, leſt the mice ſhould go into the hive
through them †. Each hole ſhould ſcarce exceed a quarter of an inch in heighth and in
wideneſs. This ſize muſt be exactly attended
to. The whole hive ſhould then be covered all
over with a large quantity of pob tow, or ſtraw,
which may be fixed to the hive with ropes made
of ſtraw, or hay. A large *divot*, or turf, ſhould
be laid upon the top of the tow or ſtraw, to
hold it cloſe down to the hive, and keep the
bees dry and warm. Afterwards, ſome of the

N   tow

† Mice are moſt pernicious enemies to bees; for when they
get into a hive, they not only eat the honey, but the combs and
eggs, and even the bees themſelves. I am perſuaded there are hundreds of hives deſtroyed every year in Britain by theſe vermin. I
myſelf, in my younger years, had no fewer than five hives ruined
in one winter by theſe rapacious invaders : but now, by taking
care to have the entries to my hives made no larger than will
juſt admit the largeſt bee, my hives are proof againſt their depredations, and I never loſe either a ſingle bee or a particle of
honey by them. The only chance the mice have, when this precaution is obſerved, is to gnaw through the hive itſelf, which
they will ſometimes attempt ; but in this they may eaſily be detected and defeated, by taking off the covering now and then.

During the cold months, ſmall ſnails often creep into the hives,
and lurk about the inſides of them, though not among the combs :
but I never obſerved that they did much hurt. When the hives
are turned up in winter to diſcover their ſtate, it is eaſy to diſ-
lodge them, and large ſnails cannot get into the hives, when the
entries are made ſmall.

tow or ftraw, fhould be rolled up about four inches above the entry, which will permit the bees to get in thereat ; for the lefs that is un-covered of the hive, the drier and warmer it will be, which fhould be aimed at in all feafons, efpecially in winter.

The beft of all covers for hives, however, that I have yet feen or heard of, are fuch as I ordered a potter to make for me of burnt earth-en ware. They are made in the form of a hive, pretty ftrong, about 21 inches wide, and 12 deep ; with a circular edging turned up at the fkirts, and a fpout about an inch in length. Thefe, being placed above the pob tow, or ftraw, keep it clofe to the hive, and may eafily be tak-en off or put on at pleafure. The fpout be-ing placed behind, all the water runs off at the back of the hive. The hives, when thus co-vered, may be compared to a man's head with a wig and hat upon it ; the pob tow refembling the wig, and the earthen cover the hat. The only objection to thefe covers is, that they are brittle, and eafily broken ; but the care, that every good bee-mafter will readily beftow upon his hives in any cafe, is fufficient to preferve them from accidents of this kind. I fold a-bove 30 of thefe covers to a gentleman in Nor-thumberland

thumberland about three years ago, and I have
reafon to believe that there is not one of them
yet broken.

C H A P. XIV.

HOW TO MANAGE BEES IN WINTER.

THE hives in September, being properly placed, covered, and made fit to endure the winter,
there is very little more neceffary to be done,
for about three months. This feafon may,
therefore, be called *the Bee-mafter's refling time.*
It will be proper, however, occafionally to take
care, that the covers continue to ftand firmly
upon the hives, and that no mice neftle about
them. When the froft is fevere, or when fnow
is lying on the ground, it will be neceffary to
prevent the bees from coming out of the hives,
by fhutting up their entry quite clofe with pob-
tow ; which will keep them warm, at the fame
time that they will run no rifk of fuffocation in

N 2   very

very cold weather.* In extreme colds, the hives
may be taken into out-houfes, which will preserve

---

* Bees fhould by no means be difturbed in cold weather, fo
as to provoke them to go abroad out of their hives, unlefs fome
very important object is in view: For, not only in winter, but
even in fpring, fummer and autumn, if they fly out of their hives
in cold or wet days, efpecially in the evenings or mornings, and
alight on the ground, their active powers become inftantly fo
benumbed, that often within half a minute thereafter, they
will be rendered totally unable to rife, in confequence of
which they muft crawl about till they perifh. If bees are permitted to go abroad in time of fnow, which they are tempted to
do, by the glare of the light, they will alight upon it, and fip a
little; but their delicate bodies are foon fo chilled by the cold,
that their wings lofe their power of raifing them, and inevitable
death fucceeds.

Every other part of the hive, as well as the entry, fhould be
carefully examined, to difcover if it be all quite clofe; for after
long confinement, efpecially when the feafon is advanced fo a-
bout the middle of February, the bees will make every poffible
attempt to get out of the hive, as their own ordure then becomes
offenfive to them. At times, when I have thought the entry to
the hive was made fo completely fecure, that not a fingle bee
could get out at any opening, yet, in walking through my apiary,
I have difcovered them making their way through places, where
I could not have fuppofed they would have attempted an efcape.
When bees are completely fhut up in a good clofe hive, they are
in a ftate of perfect darknefs; but, if there be the fmalleft aperture in any part of it, the light, fhining through it, leads them
directly to the place; when they are apt to make every poffible
effort to widen it, and, in fuch cafes, they will often fqueeze
through

ferve them from cold. But, indeed, when the hives are properly covered, and the entries to them clofely fhut up, they will refift a very fevere cold.

Many ingenious gentlemen have tried different methods to preferve bees in winter. Some have fhut them up in cold out-houfes, from September to April; others only from the 1ft of November to March. A third clafs place grates before their entries, to admit air, but keep the bees clofe in their hives, during the whole winter.

The limits of this performance will not permit me to enlarge upon the fruitleffnefs of thefe inventions. Suffice it therefore to obferve

through a very narrow hole. It is therefore advifeable, though the hives may be fuppofed perfectly clofe, to infpect them frequently, left any bees fhould get out at an unfufpected place, and not only perifh themfelves, but leave an opening for invaders to get in. Befides, upon returning to their hives, they will go to their ufual entry to get in again, and not finding admittance, will wander about in fearch of it, till they perifh, unlefs they chance to alight upon the aperture by which they had got out. The fame caution muft be obferved, when a hive is fhut up at any other feafon of the year, or upon any account whatever.

I have fometimes picked up great numbers of wandering bees from off the cold ground, or fnow, and, after recovering them by gradual warmth, have reftored them again to their hives.

ferve in general, that long confinement is prejudicial to the health of the bees; and that, as
they do eat a little during their confinement,
it is neceffary that they fhould get out to void
their ordure; for, I have even feen bees, in
fome hives that have been long confined, fwell-
ed to fuch a fize, for want of fuch opportunities, that they feemed larger than a Queen bee;
and, when they did at laft get liberty to go
out of their hives, being unable to fly, they
would fall over the edge of their ftool, and
creep about on the ground, till they died in
great numbers; fo that fcarce one of a dozen
of them ever recovered. But when they are
permitted to go out occafionally, in fine winter days, they get fo much benefit by the free
air, and by eafing their bodies in flying, that,
when they return to their hives, they are able
to turn out the dead bees, and they conclude
the day with a *fong*;—a fure fign that they are
healthy and happy. In fhort, I find by experience, that bees thrive beft, when the hives
are allowed to ftand out, and when the bees
are at liberty to go out and in at pleafure in
fine days, even in winter; for they are wife
enough to know when they may venture out
with fafety; and they will come to the door
of

of their hive to eafe nature, and return again, when the weather forbids their going abroad.

It is faid by many writers on this fubject, that a fine winter is dangerous to the bees, and that many more of them die in a mild winter than in a cold one. They argue, that as the appetite of the bees increafes by their going often out, they confume their provifions, and die of famine ; whereas, when long confined in their hives, they hardly eat any. * I acknowledge

---

* Some Authors, particularly Mr. Stephen White, alledge, that fevere cold is rather falutary for bees, as it keeps them in a torpid ftate, in confequence of which they eat none at all. I acknowlege, that they eat much lefs in cold weather than in warm, becaufe they have little or no exercife, and their appetite increafes or decreafes in proportion to the exercife they take. In November, December, and January, bees eat very little food, as any perfon may be convinced, by weighing their hives in the begining and the end of thefe months, when he will find very little difference in point of weight. But if he will weigh a hive in the beginning of March, and weigh it again at the end of it, he will find a confiderable decreafe ; for the bees, having now much exercife, eat more honey during that month, than during all the three above mentioned cold months ; and I am perfuaded, that they devour three times as much in May as in March, owing to the fame caufe operating in an increafing proportion. But that the bees eat *none at all* in cold weather is a great miftake, and may eafily be refuted : For let any perfon, in winter, put a number of bees into a hive that has nothing but empty combs,

and

knowledge, that, in a mild winter, they do eat
more food than in a cold one, when they cannot get out ; but this, as well as the fine air,
contributes greatly to their health ; besides that
they hatch earlier, and consequently increase
the number of bees in the hives sooner. The
fact is, that experience, which is preferable to
the conjectural reasoning of the most eminent
authors, may convince any person, that many
more bees die in severe winters than in mild
ones. In winter 1776 which was very cold,
a great number of Bee-hives perished ; and also
during last winter, (1794-5) being an excessive-
ly

and let them be kept equally cold with those in hives that contain both honey and bees, and a trial of eight or ten days will
convince him, that *honey,* and not *cold,* is the proper food of
bees.

In the very midst of a severe frost, I have often seen my hives
with young broods in them ; a sure sign, that they were neither motionless, nor in a state of inactivity. This fact also proves
how greatly mistaken many authors are, who assert, that bees do
not breed, till they begin to carry home loads in spring. I am
confident, that there is not a month in the whole year, in which
I have not seen many of my hives, with some eggs as well as
young bees in the cells ; although there are at least four months
in the year in which the bees carry home no loads. I will allow, however, that although they do breed some in winter, the
number is very small. Perhaps the Queen does not lay above
three or four eggs in a day, whereas in summer she will lay daily
above a hundred.

ly fevere one, many hives were deſtroyed from
that cauſe alone; whereas in winter 1779, which
was remarkably mild, not one hive in twenty
failed; and the bees, in general, ſwarmed a
month earlier than uſual.*

I have ſeen the bees of a hive that had been
long confined by cold, (perhaps for ten weeks,)

O   ſo

---

* Mr Wildman ſays, page 249, " The degree of cold, which
" bees can endure has not been aſcertained. We find that they
" live in the cold parts of Ruſſia, and often in hollow-trees,
" without any care being taken of them." Page 252, he ſays,
" that bees ſuffer ſuch degrees of cold, as we here are ſtrangers
" to, without detriment, ſeems certain; nor is it eaſily accounted
" for, why a much leſs degree of cold becomes fatal to them
" in our mild climate. If I may venture my opinion, I think
" that in theſe extreme colds, the bees are ſo perfectly frozen,
" that their juices cannot corrupt or putrify but they remain in the
" ſame ſtate till the return of ſpring; when the change of the
" weather being ſudden, the bees ſoon come to life; whereas in
" our climate they are ſo far chilled as to loſe the ſigns of life,
" and their juices being ſtill in a liquid ſtate, ſoon putrify, and
" real death enſues with corruption."

With all due deference, I ſhall now venture to give my opinion, on this point. I would account for it in this manner; that
the ſame *degree* of cold will prove equally fatal to bees in Britain, Russia, Siberia, or any other place in the world; and
that whenever the cold is ſo great, as to render the bees entirely *motionleſs*, they will continue in that ſtate for ever; or,
in other words, they will *die*; unleſs they be recovered by heat,

before

ſo diſeaſed, that, when good weather returned, and they came abroad, very great numbers would have died within a day or two thereafter ; and the hive in general would have been greatly reduced.   It is evident, that their long
confinement

before putrifaction takes place, which will otherwiſe happen within two days at moſt, after they are frozen.   Laſt winter (1794-5) it was perhaps as cold here, at leaſt for one week during the ſtorm, as it is in Ruſſia or Siberia, in ſome moderate winters.   Some of our bees were, at that period, as completely and irrecoverably frozen, during thoſe eight days, as ever any hive could be in Ruſſia ; and all the heat that human power could apply, however gradual or moderate, could not have recovered them to life again.

As a proof of this, any perſon may make the following experiment : Take a bee, during a hard froſt, and lay it upon a ſtone ; within two minutes it will be frozen, and to all appearance dead.   If it ly on the ſtone, for ſix or eight hours, it will be as completely frozen, as if it had been eight days in the coldeſt place in the world.   Yet, by warming it in a warm bed, for half an hour, it may be brought to life again ; whereas, if it be allowed to ly for eight days upon the ſame ſtone, (during which time it would be as completely frozen, as if it had been eight days in Ruſſia) neither the heat of a bed, nor any other degree of heat whatever, will ever be able to recover it.   On the whole, I am of opinion, that all poſſible care ſhould be taken to preſerve bees from ſevere cold in every corner of the world ; and I doubt much, if ever there was a ſingle hive, that was once completely frozen for twenty days, that, even in Ruſſia itſelf, or any other part of the globe, was ever recovered to life again.

confinement was the caufe ; but it is alfo certain, that, even in thofe cold countries, where
the winter lafts eight months, bees thrive and
profper well, elfe they never could produce fo
much honey*. I have known bees do well, however, that had been confined in their hives for
five months, even in this country ; while o-
thers of them were ready to perifh, by retain-
ing their fœces for fo long a period. Sometimes, about Martinmas, I have feen four hives,
ftanding in one place, all equally thriving and
numerous ; but, in confequence of having been
confined by bad weather for fix or eight weeks
after that period, one of thefe hives would have
had feveral hundreds of dead bees, lying fwoln
on the ftool, while the other three were ftill in
a thriving condition, and had fcarcely a dozen
dead bees in each. Upon tearing one of the
dead bees afunder, I found her inteftines quite
full of fœces ; which, I therefore conjectured,
was

---

* The reafon may be acounted for in this manner : fuppofe, for
inftance, that one fourth part of the bees in thofe places fhould
fail by long confinement or fevere colds, (from which I fuppofe
the natives will guard their bees as much as poffible,) yet the
remaining three parts will increafe greatly in bees and honey during their fummer, as the weather is very conftant and warm
while the honey feafon lafts.

was the caufe of her death; whereas the inteftines of the thriving bees had very little matter in them, and therefore, I am inclined to
think that this was the reafon of their continuing healthy and active. Whether the original difeafe of the former clafs, and their pre-
mature deaths, proceeded from their gluttony,
in gormandizing more food than was neceffary; or whether it was an epidemical difeafe
that had got in among them, and carried them
off in fuch numbers, I will not prefume to determine; though I rather incline to the former
opinion. But, from whatever caufe the difeafe
proceeds, fuch hives often lofe their inhabitants at the rate of a dozen' or more *per* day,
till they are greatly reduced, or perhaps quite
defolated at laft.

For fuch misfortunes, I know of no remedy
or even preventative; but it is fortunate, that
fcarcely one or two hives of a dozen meet
with them. Sometimes I have united the living
bees, that remained of fuch a hive, with thofe
of a healthy one, but feldom found it turn
out well; owing perhaps to this caufe, that the
difeafe was really contagious, and the difeafed
bees might carry the infection along with
them, and thereby hurt the healthy hive. I
generally,

generally, therefore, let the remaining bees of fuch an unfortunate hive, take their chance; and on the firft favourable day allow them to fly about, and difcharge their burdens, which muft doubtlefs enable them to return to the hive with a greater degree of health; but I am confident that many of the difeafed ones never return, and indeed the hive will be fully as well without them.

About the middle of January, every hive may be gently lifted off the ftool, and the ftate of it examined. The ftool fhould then be carefully cleanfed of dead bees, or any filth that may have gathered upon it during the winter. The hive fhould then be replaced upon the ftool, and carefully plaftered about the fkirts again, and covered over as formerly. If the bees of any hive have deferted it, and gone into another, which they fometimes do, (as fhall be further noticed in a fubfequent chapter,) the hive may be carefully kept, in order to feed bees with the honey it contains in fpring, or to receive a young fwarm in fummer.

CHAP

CHAP. XV.

DIRECTIONS HOW TO SUPLY BEES WITH FOOD.

As bees fometimes run fhort of provifions, ef-pecially when there is a long continuance of cold or wet weather, during Spring, or even in the be-ginning of Summer, it is abfolutely neceffary to re-inforce the hives, efpecially the light ones, with additional ftore. There are four methods of fupplying the hives in fuch cafes, which I fhall lay before the reader, and one or other of which, every bee-mafter fhould attend to, at fuch feafons, of the year as he finds his bees will need a re-inforcement of provifion.

I. The firft, and indeed the beft method is by *ecking**. Take an eek,* of fix or eight rows deep, and place it on a ftool, with the quanti-ty

** To *eek*, in the Scotch dialeft, fignifies literally to *add* to any thing. The *eek*, or *addition* here meant, is a part of an old hive, cut down on purpofe, to give room for placing the fupply of provifion under the deficient hive.

ty of honey, neceſſary to ſupply the deficient
hive, within it, which may be from one to
four, or even eight pounds of honey, according to the deficiency that appears, and the
number of bees in the hive. The combs
ſhould be placed in the eek, in ſuch a poſition,
that the bees may have free acceſs to the honey,
on all ſides. At night, let the deficient hive be
gently placed upon the eek, and let the inter-
ſtices between the hive and the eek be plaſter-
ed up with lime ; after which let the entry be
ſhut, that neither native bees nor ſtrangers
may get acceſs. Let the hive and the eek continue in this ſituation for 24 hours ; in which
time the bees will have removed all the looſe
particles of the honey, and the ſmell of it will
not be ſo apt to invite ſtrange bees. The entry at the bottom of the eek may, therefore,
now be opened, and the bees allowed free e-
greſs and acceſs. If the additional quantity of
honey given in the eek did not exceed a pound
or two, the eek may be removed within three
or four days ; but if it amounted to ſix or eight
pounds, it may be allowed to remain for ſix
weeks in Spring. ‡ If, in September, a hive
has

* This method may be practiſed at all ſeaſons of the year,
and

has got an additional supply of twelve or sixteen pounds, it should be allowed to remain at least as many weeks, if not altogether ; only at this season, place all the combs in the eek, in the same order in which they were naturally in the hive they were taken from ;—the uppermost cells to be still upermost, and so of the rest, leaving a space of an inch and a half between the combs. The combs must be fixed with sticks to make them stand on their edges, and they should run as much in the same direction as possible, with those in the hive. The bees will soon join the combs together, and render them fit to be lifted all at once. In Spring, if the original hive be large, the eek and combs may be removed, but if small, they should both remain during Summer.

II.

and it has this additional advantage, that it may be executed at little expence, and occasion a saving of all the honey in the old combs that will not run out, or that happens to be mixed with bee-bread, eggs, or young bees. All such honey ought to be thrown into these *granaries*, and the bees will soon carry up all the honey, and place it in their own reservoirs, leaving only the empty combs, which can be melted and made into wax afterwards. It need hardly be added, that the bees do not, in such cases, instantly eat all the additional honey that is given them, but only lay it up for future use.

II. The second method is the same with the preceding, but differs only in this particular; that when the Bee-master has no old combs with honey in them, he must melt fresh honey, and pour it into large empty combs, of which drone combs are the best, and place them into the eek as above directed.

III. The third method is, to save the trouble of eeking the hive, (when a small quantity may serve,) by placing a comb, with melted honey in it, upon the stool, immediately before the entry of the deficient hive, and leaving it entirely to the industry of the bees, to collect and carry it into the hive. The only disadvantage of this method is, that strange bees will be tempted to molest the natives, in consequence of which a battle may ensue, and some lives may be lost. But, to prevent this, let the honey be given at a time of the day when no bees are abroad, and the danger will be avoided. I have sometimes had a dozen of hives in one apiary, with a feeding comb placed before each; which gave all the bees of each hive so much employment at their own doors, that they had neither time nor inclination to molest or rob their neighbours.

IV. The fourth method is, to turn up the

P   deficient

deficient hive, and, laying it on one fide, to pour melted honey into the empty cells, where there are few or no bees; and, when the one fide of all the combs are properly filled, to turn up the other, and fill their empty cells with honey alfo. A tea-pot is moft proper for executing this plan. In this manner I have fometimes poured two pounds of honey into a hive at a time. When the hive is again placed on the ftool, a little honey will run down from the combs upon it; but the entry being clofe fhut up, will prevent robbers from fmelling the treafure, and will keep fuch bees, as may have been befmeared with honey during the operation, within the hive. The native bees will foon not only lick up all the fpilt honey from the ftool, but will alfo fuck it off the backs of their befmeared brethren, and lay it up in their refervoirs, with fo much expedition, that next day not a drop of it will be vifible, either on the ftool or on the bodies of the bees.

It is not to be doubted, that, in cafes of neceffity, bees may be fed and preferved with other articles, befides honey; fuch as fugar, fweet wort, treacle and the like : but I am of opinion, that they cannot be fed, either at lefs expence or with as much fafety, with any other thing

than

than their own natural food. To give them any other fubftitute, would occafion as much expence, and a great deal of more trouble, efpecially when the hives are well filled with inhabitants : and I dare venture to fay, that as fuch methods have never yet been much adopted, fo, if ever they fhould, they will not turn out to the proprietors advantage, or become of general ufe, in the prefervation of bees. But it muft be owned, that, if no honey can be obtained to feed bees with, in fpring, fome of the above fubftitutes will fupply the deficiency tolerably well. In fuch a cafe, let 1 lb. of brown fugar be mixed with half a gill, (or half a quartern) of fmall beer, and let a table fpoonful at a time be placed before the entry to the hive, as above recommended in the third method. Let this be repeated daily as long as is neceffary, and the hive will be preferved from famine, and will in all probability do well; but when a hive is light in September, it ought to be fupplied with nothing but honey.

CHAP.

C H A P. XVI.

OF THE WARS AND ROBBERIES THAT TAKE PLACE AMONG THE
BEES.

IT cannot be denied, that the animals, who
are the subject of this treatise, have their *vices*,
as well as their *virtues*. To the virtues of *industry* and *oeconomy*, which they are endued
with in an eminent degree, we must add, what
some would call a *martial spirit*, but which rather deserves to be denominated, a spirit of
theiving and *robbery*. For when the weather is
good, and there are not flowers in the fields
for the bees to work on, they will risk their
lives by robbing other hives, and strive to enrich their own hive at the expence and ruin of
their neighbours. In such cases, the hives
that are thinly inhabited, are ready to fall a
prey to the bold invaders; for hardly one hive
within their reach is left unassaulted; and as,
among mankind, the strong overpower and

subjugate

subjugate the weak, so a weak hive sometimes
falls a prey to a set of strong invaders; but
when strong and *populous* hives (so to speak,)
are attacked by a less numerous body of robbers, they give them a terrible reception, and
hardly a single bee, that they can get hold of,
gets off to tell his neighbours the fate of his
brethren. Sometimes a good number of hives
will join in robbing one single hive. In such
a case, all is confusion and rage, and great
slaughter takes place. The bees are seen flying in the air like so many fiery dragons ready
to attack every one; and whoever dares ob-
struct their flight, will feel their poisonous
spears in a moment. At such a time, one dare
scarcely venture near them, unless he is resolv-
ed to receive wounds from all quarters. When
they are engaged thus, their sound in the air
is easily distinguished.

The people's actions will their thoughts declare,
All their hearts tremble, and beat thick for war.
Hoarse broken sounds, like trumpets harsh alarms,
Run through the hive, and call them forth to arms:
All in a hurry spread their shiv'ring wings,
And fit their claws, and point their angry stings:
In crouds before the hive they all do light,
And boldly challenge out the foe to fight.
VIRGIL.

Various reasons have been assigned for this propensity of the bees to rob one another. A majority of writers impute it to the following causes :

1*st*, The scarcity of provisions : The bees of one hive, finding they have not sufficient provision for themselves, and the season being backward, try to enrich themselves at the expence of their neighbours.

2*dly*, The artificial feeding of hives : When one hive is fed, their neighbours, smelling the fresh honey, wish for a share of it, and will take no denial, though it should cost them their lives : which it often does, the inhabitants of the fed hives standing up most heroically in defence of their property. This consideration will lead the attentive Bee-master to study the utmost caution and prudence in feeding such hives as require extra supplies ; else the remedy will prove worse than the disease.

3*dly*, But the chief reason is, their insatiable avarice for honey.— In spring and autumn, when the weather is good, but little or no honey can be collected from plants, all bees whatsoever are apt to go a *marauding* and plundering their neighbour's hives ; although, it must

be

be owned, the pooreft are moft addicted to pil-
fering.

Here it is neceffary to inform the reader,
how thefe robbers are to be diftinguifhed as
well as how to get rid of them. When a number of bees are feen crowding into a hive, and
many dead bees lying flaughtered before the
gates ;—when others are feen flying as if af-
frighted, and the native bees purfuing, catching, wreftling, and buftling with them upon
the ftool, in a moft furious manner, then it
may be fafely inferred that robbers are attack-
ing the hive; which indeed, if it be weak in
numbers, will not be worth preferving. In
that cafe, the beft way will be, to turn up the
hive, and diflodge the robbers by rapping upon
it, and at night to put the bees belonging to
it into any other hive that will receive them.
The manner of doing this will be taken notice
of, when we come to mention the beft mode of
re-inforcing a hive. But if the hive that is
attacked be tolerably full of valiant bees, who
withftand their foes ftoutly, then let the entry
be made fo fmall, that only one bee can get in
at once, and let fome perfon ftand before the hive
with a light cloth in his hand, to wave the robbers afide, and keep them off, till a fhower of
rain,

rain, or night coming on, or perhaps a dark cloud intercepting the fun's rays, oblige the invaders to retreat. Next morning, if the weather be good, let the hive be fhut up clofe, to prevent the robbers from getting accefs; and let it continue fo for fome time, till the invaders give over their attempt; but if they continue their inroads daily, let the hive be removed to the diftance of a mile or fo; and indeed this is the moft effectual method to free the hive from farther moleftation.

In my younger years, thefe robberies gave me much uneafinefs, as I was alarmed at the fight of a flaughtered bee; but now I give myfelf no concern, as I either put the bees of the hive that is attacked into another hive, or remove them to a proper diftance from danger. I have frequently, indeed, feen fome fore battle take place among my own bees, and laft for perhaps a day or two; after which a peace would have enfued, without my interference. But good hives feldom fuffer much by robberies; perhaps not one in fifty. They may indeed lofe a fcore of bees or fo, but that will never hurt them.

CHAP.

CHAP. XVII.

DIRECTIONS HOW TO MANAGE BEES IN MARCH, APRIL, AND
MAY.

In fpring, hives are fometimes found without
a fingle bee in them, and the owner, in fuch
cafes, is at a lofs to account for the caufe.
The following circumftance, which occurred.
among my own bees, will throw fome light on
this fubject.

The long continuance of the late ftorm
(1794-5) having confined the bees in their
hives for about four months, the bees of fome
hives contracted difeafes, which, during the
laft month of their confinement proved very
fatal to them; and fome of them daily fell
down, or rather *came* down of their own ac-
cord, from the combs to the ftool, in fearch of
fome aperture to get out at, in order to void
their fœces; but, after crawling about on the
bottom of the hive for a confiderable time in

Q   vain

vain, the cold benumbed them fo much, that they could not return to their brethren again, and thus death enfued. Now, fuppofing only three dozen of bees *per* day to have come down upon this errand, and perhaps not a third of them to have been able to return, it is evident, that fuch hives muft of courfe be foon greatly reduced in the number of their inhabitants. This made me anxious for good weather, that my difeafed and diftreffed fervants might get out, and recover their health, by flying about and getting rid of their fuperfluous matter. The long wifhed for period at laft arrived. The ftorm broke, and the weather became mild ; and, upon examining my hives, I found, that out of fourteen, which I had in one apiary, there were twelve whofe bees were in a healthy ftate ; and that thofe of the remaining two were partly difeafed. The day being very fine, and the doors of my hives opened, the bees flew about as thick as hail, making a great noife with their ufual mufic. My wife being prefent, we obferved, that the two difeaf-ed hives gradually diminifhed in the number of their bees, whereupon I faid, that I fuppofed the bees would foon defert thefe hives altogether ; to which fhe replied, that fhe wifh-

ed

ed they would, and that they would go into
fome other hives, provided they did not fight.
Upon farther obfervation, I found, that fome
of them entered into one hive, and fome into
another, till at laft the original hives were totally deferted, except the Queen and about a
fcore of bees; and that almoft all the bees entered into thofe hives that were moft happy,
as appeared by their making a moft harmonious found at the entry of their hives, by which
mufic they feemed to invite and welcome their
new friends. The deferted hives were well
ftored with honey, and therefore I turned
them upfide down, and placed them below
fome of my other hives, in order that the bees
might collect the honey that was in them.
Such deferted hives I have often found ufeful
for putting a young fwarm into.

I have even feen young fwarms gradually
defert their hives in this manner, and go into
other hives. When they go into one of their
own mafter's hives, I never fee any lofs by it,
efpecially when they unite peaceably; as one
good hive is worth four bad ones.

It is worthy of obfervation, that the bees, on
this occafion, deferted the weak hives gradually, and not in a body, as they do when they

fwarm

fwarm ; and alfo, that it may happen at particular times, that different men's bees, ftanding in the fame apiary, or near each other, may
join together.   Therefore, to prevent fuch circumftances from taking place, to the prejudice
of others, it is neceffary to allot a proper diftance between one man's hives and thofe of a-
nother.

Thofe who live in places where vegetation
is generally late, if they take the trouble to remove their hives to more early fituations, efpecially if they have a great number of them,
will foon find themfelves doubly repaid for
their trouble and expence, as their bees will
thereby both breed and fwarm much earlier.
I would indeed advife every bee-mafter, who
conveniently can, to keep two apiaries, an early and a late one, in confequence of which, his
bees will be conftantly employed, when the
weather is favourable, during the whole working feafon.

In fpring I generally fhut up the doors of
my hives every evening, as foon as the bees
are all got in, and open them again next morning ; and I even do this for whole days during
that feafon, when the cold is fevere ; as cold
winds blowing in at their entries are extremely

ly prejudicial to them, and ought therefore to be prevented with all poffible care. By this fimple practice, the bees are kept warm and healthy, which is greatly beneficial to them in breeding. But in following this plan, great caution muft be obferved, that the bees have no other vent to get out at, as the confequences would be fatal. (See pages 100 and 101.)

In the beginning of March, if the weather be good, the bees will begin to carry home loads of honey and wax. I have feldom feen them carry fo early as February, excepting in the year 1793, when I obferved feveral bees go into one of my hives, heavy loaden, fo early as the term of Candlemas; but I believe they hardly carried any more for a full month thereafter.

At this feafon, every hive ought to be again lifted, and the ftool cleaned; on which occafion, the ftate of the hive, both with regard to its provifions, and the number of its inhabitants, will be difcovered. Hives of twenty pounds weight ftand in no need of any fupply of food, and may therefore be immediately replaced upon their ftools, and covered, and their fkirts plaiftered as formerly; but, fuch as weigh only fourteen or fixteen pounds fhould

be

be reinforced with fix pounds of honey comb, as directed in page 110. Three pounds of honey will be a fufficient fupply for fuch as weigh eighteen pounds. Some hives perhaps will not exceed fourteen pounds or fo; yet, if they have few bees, they will not need to be fupplied; for, befides that they ftand in no need of it, a frefh fupply of honey would invite robbers, whom they would not be able, on account of the paucity of their numbers, to withftand. A thinly inhabited hive ought, therefore, never to be reinforced with honey, unlefs the bees are ready to perifh for want of food, which, in fuch a hive, feldom if ever happens. But a hive that is well peopled ought to be abundantly fupplied, even although there may appear to be a fufficiency of food, becaufe the fuperfluity will not be loft. The bees are faithful ftewards, and will not fail to repay their mafter's generofity with ufury. *

For

* The fupplying of bees with food, in any feafon, but efpecially in fpring, is of great advantage to them, as it cheers their fpirits, and roufes them to breed earlier than they otherwife would. I would therefore recommend to every bee-mafter, to give a little additional food, even to hives that have abundance, in order to revive and exhilarate the bees, and encourage them

to

For I am confident, that when they are fully fed, they will breed faſt, even in bad weather; whereas, if they have little proviſion of their own, and receive no extra ſupply, they will breed very ſlowly.

From this, as well as from other peculiarities in the nature of theſe inſects, it appears pretty evident, that they are endued with a high degree of free or voluntary agency, as they can breed early or late, frequently or ſeldom, at pleaſure, and according to circumſtances. All poſſible attention, therefore, ſhould be paid to the full feeding of bees in Spring, and alſo in the beginning of ſummer, if the weather be unfavourable.

A hive will ſometimes loſe their Queen in ſpring, and of courſe will go to ruin, as it will then be impoſſible for the bees to raiſe another, if they have not an egg to raiſe one from. A hive may be known to be in this ſad predicament, by the following ſymptoms : The bees will

to hatch their young families, early in the ſeaſon. But ſuch hives as weigh heavy in March or April, having plenty of honey, with bees in them carrying well, may be ſafely allowed to remain without any freſh ſupply of food, as they will proſper without it; although, if the owner has time and abundance of honey, he may reap additional profit by giving them a little.

will immediately give over working as foon as
the young in the cells are fealed up; and one
may wait an hour at the hive without feeing a
loaded bee enter it.   The bees then confume
their own honey faft, and an uncommon number of them generally croud about the entry:
And if the hive has been long without a Queen,
upon turning it up, and fearching for maggots
in the cells, they will be found quite empty.

As foon as thefe melancholy figns are obferved, the owner fhould directly take out all the
bees, and unite them with thofe of fome other
hive, that has few bees in it, the manner of
doing which will be afterwards mentioned:
and if the hive be young, it may be kept to
put a young fwarm into, but if old, the honey
fhould be laid afide for ufe.

Sometimes, in fpring, I have found, in particular cells in hives, a confiderable number of
young that, from fome caufe or other, had decayed and never come to perfection, as mentioned, page 64.   I have fometimes obferved
the number of thefe fo great, that in one comb,
containing perhaps 600 young bees, the one
half would have been in this ftate in the cells.
The effluvia proceeding from thefe abortive
productions, gave the hive a favour by no
means

means agreeable to me, and which muft doubt
lefs have been very difgufting to the bees. I
have often endeavoured to inveftigate the caufe
of thefe phænomena, but am as yet unable to
fatisfy myfelf, unleſs perhaps it be owing to
extreme cold. But againſt this fuppofition the
objection naturally arifes, that fome eggs in the
fame hive, and in the fame degree of cold, produce bees which arrive at full maturity ; and,
therefore, in reply, it muft be taken for granted, that fome eggs are naturally more able to
bear cold than others ; and, indeed, it is moft
commonly in hives that are but thinly inhabited, that fuch misfortunes take place.

To diftinguifh hives in this condition, therefore, the following criterion may ferve. In
fpring, when bees, which formerly carried well,
and ftill are in no want of food, give over carrying, let the hive be directly turned up, and
infpected between the combs. Then, upon taking a fmall ftick, and putting it down among the
thickeft of the bees, where the maggots lie fealed up, and with it rubbing off the tops of two
or three of the fealed cells, if frefh whitifh
maggots appear, it may be concluded, that the
brood is coming forward : but if the cells appear quite empty, or if only blanched maggots

R

appear in a number of them, then it is certain that the brood is going backward.

If such a hive has but few bees, it will be proper to unite them with another hive; but if it has a confiderable number of bees, they fhould be allowed to continue to work on, in the beft way they can, till the beginning of June, when the ftrong hives begin to lay out; at which time a great number of common bees fhould be taken from one or two of them, to re-inforce that hive with, in the manner that fhall be afterwards pointed out. I have feen a hive, with a vaft number of fuch rotten eggs and decayed maggots in it, in April, which, when allowed to remain till June, and being re-inforced with frefh bees, would have turned out a fine thriving hive before autumn; although many of the decayed eggs and maggots would have ftill been in it: For I believe fome fuch abortions may continue in a hive for years, perhaps with little detriment to the bees; for they in time dry up, and wither away in the cells, and their bad favour gradually goes off. Such hives, however, fhould always be taken in autumn; and their bees united to more thriving hives. *

In

* Formerly I ufed to cut out the combs containing the moft
rotten

In May, if cold, misty, or cloudy weather, continues for a few days, the bee-master should pay particular attention to his hives, lest any of them should be in danger of famine; for, at this period, the number of bees in each hive is greatly increased, and of course they quickly consume the remains of their winter and spring provision, so that even the very best of hives will be in danger. When such weather occurs, therefore, in May or even in June, let every hive get some additional food, in order to prevent all danger of famishing, now that they are just upon the brink of their honey harvest. For, as soon as the mustard blossoms, and the white clover appear on the lees, they will make the very air to smell

R 2 of

rotten eggs, and the most decayed maggots, whereby I cleared the hive of a great nuisance, which I thought it would be much the better of wanting. But, in doing this, I found that the removal of such masses of combs occasioned a large vacancy in the hive, and thereby made it colder. To remedy this defect, I have some times put a piece of fresh comb in its place, in which I found the Queen soon laid eggs again. But still, as in these combs, containing the decayed eggs and maggots, there could not be fewer than one third, or perhaps one half of live young, intermixed among the abortions, which thus inevitably perished, I began to regret the loss of so many industrious servants thus destroyed, when just emerging into existence; and have, therefore, now laid the practice almost entirely aside.

of honey, which will make the bees eager of
work during the day, and fing for joy through
the night.   Now is the honey feafon, and farewell famine and robbers ; for, when there is
honey in the flowers, they will not rob for it ;
and, a fingle hour of a fine day will refrefh
them, and put a period to the labour of feeding them, as formerly hinted.

When the flowers begin to open, the bees
will vifit them, and carry off their yellow loads
from them.   When a loaded bee is feen going
into a hive, it is a fign that the flowers are
beginning to fpring ; and, on every fine day
during fpring, fummer, and autumn, they
continue to carry on the beloved labour, with
the utmoft diligence and alacrity.

The firft day in fpring, that I obferve a bee
carrying a load, I generally call my family together, to take a glafs, and rejoice with me
and my faithful fervants at the return of the
falutiferous feafon.   The firft day, perhaps, only three or four loaded bees are to be feen ;
the next day, probably eight or ten ; the third,
fifteen ; and fo on, the numbers ftill gradually increafing, in proportion to the increafe of
the flowers in the fields.   The bees then grow

numerous

numerous in the hives; and, about the beginning of May, when the furze and broom, and many other flowers, make the fields look yellow, a ſtrong hive of bees will be all yellow loaded; and, at ſuch a period, in a fine day, I have counted 100 loaded bees go into one hive in a few minutes.

When the hives are all equally good, the bees carry much alike, but in proportion to their number. In an apiary, where there are four hives, one will perhaps have twenty entering into it, in five minutes; another fifty, a third ninety, and the fourth a hundred and twenty, all within the ſame ſpace of time. But in the height of the honey ſeaſon, the bees carry amazingly faſt, running out and in to the hive with the moſt ſurpriſing celerity and expedition. At this period, the number of loaded bees conſtantly flocking into the hive, as well as their rapidity, defies all power of calculation; for although they labour with great aſſiduity and conſtancy before this ſeaſon, yet they do not appear to work with ſuch incredible quickneſs, as after the honey ſeaſon commences §.

If

§ In ſpring, as the bees gradually increaſe in numbers, their entry ſhould be gradually widened, leſt they ſhould be impeded

If I were intending to purchafe a hive in May, and came to an apiary where there were four hives, to make choice of one, I would defire four men to fit down for ten minutes, one at each hive, and count the number of loaded bees that entered into their refpective hives in that fpace of time; and according to their report, I would pitch upon the hive that was moft frequented during that interval, provided it had honey, and were not one of the oldeft.

CHAP.

peded in their labours; but this fhould only be done in proportion to the number of bees in a hive. During March and April, they fhould be very little, as warmnefs is health to bees, and farthers their hatching greatly. A numerous hive fhould, in May, have an entry two inches wide, and half an inch deep, while a hive, that has not perhaps half the number of bees, fhould have its entry only one inch wide and fcarcely half an inch deep. But in the midft of fummer, when the weather is warm, and the bees numerous, the entries of all the hives fhould be widened, as the bees ought to have both fufficient room to go out and in, and as much air as poffible. In fuch hot weather, the entries might even be enlarged to three inches in widenefs, and one inch in height. The method of enlarging or ftraitening the entries of hives is quite fimple. Pieces of wood, all of one fize outwardly, but with holes cut in the under part of them, of the various dimenfions above defcribed, might be made and kept ready at all times, to be exchanged with each other, according as the feafon requires, or the Bee-mafter wifhes to widen or to ftraiten his hives; but indeed a little plafter lime will ftraiten or widen an entry in fpring and fummer, with very little trouble.

CHAP. XVIII.

HOW TO UNITE OR RE-INFORCE BEE-HIVES.

As the uniting or re-inforcing of bees is often neceſſary to be performed during the ſame ſeaſon of the year, that they naturally ſend off young ſwarms, theſe two ſubjeɗs will often fall to be occaſionally intermingled in ſuch a manner, that the one cannot be particularly deſcribed without taking notice of the other. But as each article is of too much importance, not to require a ſeparate chapter, and of courſe a *precedence* to one of them, I ſhall firſt deſcribe the UNITING or RE-INFORCING of bee-hives, as it is often neceſſary in different ſeaſons of the year, and ſhall devote a ſubſequent chapter or two to the ſubjeɗ of SWARMING.

In handling bees at all times, but eſpecially when driving them, or managing a ſwarm, gentleneſs and boldneſs are equally neceſſary.

Every

Every motion muſt be made deliberately, and without hurry. The operator may take a glaſs of good ale, and rub ſome of it over his face and hands ; but during the whole operation he muſt be particularly careful not to bruiſe any of the bees..

In uniting and re-inforcing bees,* upon the very

* To RE-INFORCE a hive, ſignifies to take part of the bees out of a ſtrong hive, and put them into a weak or deficient one, in order to ſtrengthen it, and make it a thriving hive. But one thing to be obſerved here, is, that no bees muſt ever be taken from a ſtock hive to re-inforce another with, unleſs in ſummer, when the hive is ſo full of bees as to lay out, or nearly ſo ; for no good hive ought at any time to be hurt to enrich a weak one. It is often a very neceſſary and uſeful operation, when a hive has few bees in ſummer, by re-inforcing her from a more numerous hive that can eaſily ſpare them, the weak hive will ſoon become ſtrong. Or ſhould a misfortune befal a hive at any ſeaſon of the year, the bees of the unfortunate hive ſhould be put into another hive ; and in September, all the bees belonging to the hives which are taken, ſhould be put into the ſtock hives, whereby they will preſerve heat through the winter, and be able to accelerate their labours in the ſpring.

In all caſes whatſoever, where it is neceſſary to remove the bees out of one hive into another, the new hive muſt be placed in the ſame ſpot where the old hive ſtood, to prevent the bees from miſtaking it. But when a hive is re-inforced by an additional number of bees, if theſe bees are taken from three or four different hives, ſituated in as many different places, the re-inforced hive ſhould be removed about a mile diſtant from all of them, to prevent the new inhabitants from returning to their original hives

again ;

very beft plan that I know of, they will fometimes fight a little ; but, although I cannot abfolutely prevent this inconvenience, nor indeed
have I ever met with any author, or feen any
perfon, who could take in hand to do it, yet I
can ufe fuch means, as will probably prevent
any conflict from taking place in one of a dozen
of thefe operations ; and, although a few battles
may occur among fome individual bees, yet
in general very few will be killed on either
fide. I am, therefore, never afraid to unite
them, when I have reafon to believe it will anfwer a good purpofe in other refpects. But,
in all cafes of uniting bees, particular care
fhould be taken firft to try the deficient hive
with a fpecimen of the bees that are intended
to be introduced into it ; and if thefe *ambaffadors* are gracioufly received, the reft of their
brethren may be fafely offered : But, if otherwife, the whole of the bees fhould be kept
back, till thofe of the receiving hive fhall be in

S

better

again. But after ftanding fix weeks, it may be returned back to
its former fituation. The above general directions, I think abfolutely neceffary to be obferved, in driving, re-inforcing, and
fwarming of bees ; and I am perfuaded they will anfwer in moft
cafes, though particular circumftances may occur, wherein the
practical bee-mafter's judgment muft direct him ; as it is impoffible
to anticipate every contingency, in a limited work of this nature,

better humour; for, it is to be remarked, that
the fame bees will often fight at one time, who
will unite in the moſt kindly manner at another; on which account the receiving hive
ſhould always be previouſly tried, with a ſpecimen of their intended new aſſociates.

To drive all the bees out of a hive, at any
feaſon of the year, either to re-inforce another
hive, or to raiſe an artificial ſwarm, the hive
muſt be gently turned up, and the top of it
placed in an eek, or in a hole made in the
ground on purpoſe, to prevent it from being
overturned. An empty hive of the ſame ſize
muſt then be gently placed over it, mouth to
mouth, and a ſheet, or large cloth, wrapped round
the joinings of the hives, to prevent any of the
bees from getting out. The undermoſt hive
muſt then be rapped with both hands in the
manner a drum is beat; rapping chiefly on thoſe
parts of the hive to which the edges of the
combs are fixed, and avoiding the parts oppo-
ſite to the ſides of the combs, left they ſhould
be looſened, and, by falling together, cruſh the
bees between them, as well as the young in
the cells. Even the Queen herſelf might be
in danger of ſuffering. By not adverting to
this, I have ſeen the looſe combs and bruiſed

bees

bees fall out upon turning up the hive, all of
which are a confiderable·lofs. The older any
hive is, there is the lefs danger of loofening
the combs ; and the more bees there are in it,
the fooner they will run into the new hive ;
for the concuffion of the hive, by the rapping,
alarms them, as an earthquake alarms mankind, and they run to the upper hive in fearch
of a more fafe habitation. Thofe that enter
firft, finding themfelves fafe, invite their brethren by their founding to follow them, which
they quickly do. The fheet may then be removed, and the edge of the upper hive next the
right hand lifted up, when, upon a narrow infpection, the Queen fometimes will be obferved to go up along with the reft.

When all the bees are thus removed into the
new hive, it may be placed where the old one
ftood, which will collect all the bees together,
and within ten minutes, they will fall a working as bufily as any natural fwarm.

It is neceffary, before this operation, to remove
the hive, eight or ten yards at leaft, from every
other hive, to prevent difturbance from other
bees. An empty hive fhould alfo be placed
where the old hive ftood, to amufe thofe bees belonging to it, that may return loaded from the

fields

fields. This operation may be very eafily performed at any hour of the day; but
the fafeft time is when they are moft bufy at
work, as they are not then fo ready to fting the
operator. In this manner, I have taken off
four artificial fwarms in one forenoon, and
hardly received a fingle fting; for the operation is quite eafily performed, efpecially in the
middle of the day. †

In

---

† Indeed, there is hardly any thing that is requifite to be
done about bees, that I would not take in hand to perform, with
fufficient time and attention.

I could put TWENTY hives, for inftance, into ONE, if neceffary:
I can caufe my bees to rear as many Queens as I pleafe: I can
rob my bees of part of their honey, at any time: I could carry
100 bee hives to LONDON or RUSSIA: I could rear 5,000 bee-
hives in a few years, if defired by any gentleman of property: I could travel through the ftreets of Edinburgh with
three fwarms of bees about me, unhurt: I can take a fwarm out of
any hive at any time: I can take 10,000 bees from ten different hives, and unite them into one hive; and I can re-inforce a weak hive with bees from any number of other hives,
and from being the WORST, make it the BEST hive in the county;
I can unite the bees of forty hives into thirty, twenty, or ten
hives; and next Summer divide thefe ten hives again into forty
fwarms: If I have a weak hive fuffering by robbers, I can
ftrengthen it with more bees, and make them fit to rob any hive
in the neighbourhood: If I have a hive of bees perifhing with
poverty or famine, I can make it the richeft hive in the place, or
within many miles around: I can take a common bee egg, and
caufe

In fummer, a weak hive, that has few inhabitants, may be re-inforced with a number of
bees from a ftrong one, in the following manner : Suppofing there are two apiaries, a mile
diftant from each other ; and that, in one of
them, there are a weak hive and a ftrong one,
fituated within two feet or two yards of each
other ; and no other hive near them : in fuch
a cafe, let the ftrong hive be removed, about
ten o'clock A. M. when the bees are bufy at
work, to twenty or thirty yards diftance, and
let the weak hive be placed where the ftrong
one ftood. All the bees, belonging to the
ftrong hive, that were abroad in the fields, will
thus, on their return, go into the weak hive and
unite peaceably with its inhabitants. Upon
this plan, fcarce one of twenty will fight ; but
if they fhould, which is feldom the cafe when
they are bufy at work, then the ftrong hive
muft be immediately brought back, and placed
in its former fituation ; and the weak hive
turned up and rapped heartily, upon which
the

caufe the bees raife it to be either a Queen or a common bee as I
pleafe : I can make my bees reft upon myfelf or any perfon near
me, without offering us the fmalleft injury ; and I can make
them fall upon us with the fury of as many dragons, fo that we
would be glad to fly with as much precipitation, as a few rioters
would do before a regiment of dragoons.

the bees will return to their own hive again;
and the weak hive may be placed in its former fituation.   But when a part of the bees
of the ftrong hive unite peaceably with thofe
of the weak one, the ftrong hive fhould
be carried to the other apiary : for fhould it
be placed too near the fituation where it formerly ftood, too many of its bees might go into
the weak hive, and thus the one be impover-
ifhed by enriching the other.   Another method, to re-inforce a hive with bees, is to bring
it into a clean room, where there is only one
window ; then turn it up, and rap upon it, till
fome hundreds of the bees fly to the light.
They will run up and down the glafs in a bewildered manner, wondering, (we may fuppofe,) how the air has become fo thick, that
they cannot pafs through it.   Let them remain
in this fituation for about twenty minutes,
which will cool their courage for fighting.
Then let three or four fcore of thofe bees, that
are wifhed to be united to them, be introduced clofe to them.   Thefe will appear as much
bewildered as the former, by the glafs preventing their egrefs, and will readily unite with
them, without killing a fingle bee.   Upon finding them thus agree, let them all be brought

to

to the window ; and a fhort time after, let the
hive be placed near them, and they will all run
into it chearfully : after which the hive, thus
re-inforced, may be placed in its former fituation, provided it be about a mile diftant from the
place where the old hive formerly ftood. Upon this plan, even all the combs may be taken
out of a hive one by one, during which time,
the bees will fly to the window, and a few of
the bees of the receiving hive being made to
join them, upon their uniting kindly, the receiving hive may be placed as above directed.

I have often re-inforced weak hives in fpring,
which have done very well, though, at other
times, they turned out very indifferently. I
therefore feldom attempt to do it now, till the
ftrong hives are full of bees, and feem to be
near fwarming : on which occafions they can
afford 2000 common bees to ftrengthen a weak
hive, with very little injury to their own.

Again, in fummer, a weak hive may be re-
inforced by changing its fituation with that of
a ftrong one, upon a fine day, when the bees
are bufily employed at work. I have often
practifed this bufinefs with much fuccefs and
fatisfaction. But, if they fhould not unite in
a friendly manner, let both be turned up, the
ftrange

ftrange bees rapped out, and each hive reſtored
to its former ſituation.

CHAP. XIX.

OF HABITATIONS PROPER FOR BEES TO LIVE AND WORK IN.

HIVES, or the habitations in which bees live,
breed and work, have been made of different
materials, and in different forms, according to
the fancy of people of different ages and countries. MELISSUS, king of Crete, is ſaid to have
been the firſt who invented and taught the uſe
of bee-hives. Not only ſtraw, which experience now proves to be rather preferable to every
thing elſe, but wood, horn, glaſs, &c. have been
uſed for the conſtruction of hives. Single box
hives, however, when properly made, anſwer
very well, and, when painted, laſt long. They
have ſeveral advantages above ſtraw hives:
They are quite cleanly, and always ſtand up-
right; they are proof againſt mice; and are
cheaper in the end than ſtraw hives; for one

box

box hive will laft as long as three of them. I
have known many bee-mafters, who never ufed any other kind of hives, and whofe bees
throve very well. I believe, however, they are
rather colder in winter, but a proper covering
will prevent all danger from that quarter. But
ftraw hives are eafieft obtained at firft, and
have been ufed and recommended by the moft
of bee-mafters.

As to the fize, a hive that will hold about $2\frac{1}{2}$
pecks, Linlithgow meafure, will hold a pretty
large fwarm ; but there is no certain rule to
judge what hive will be exactly filled by a
fwarm. Much depends upon the fucceeding
feafon. If the fwarm be early and large, it
will require a large hive ; but if otherwife, the
hive fhould be proportionably lefs. If a fwarm
be put into one of the fize above mentioned,
and the bees fill it foon, and appear to want
more room, it can eafily be enlarged, by putting an eek below it : but if it be heavy enough
for a ftock hive, it will do, although it fhould
not be quite full of combs.

A ftraw hive, when made, fhould have a
piece of wood, fixed in the undermoft roll, four
inches long, with a notch cut out of it, three
inches long, and one high, for an entry to the

bees

bees. The ftraw of rye or wheat is beft for making hives: The heads of the ftraw fhould be cut off: The rolls fhould be drawn very tight, and wrought together with fmall willows or brambles, fplit and properly dreft, with the pith taken out of them. The hives fhould be made as fmooth as poffible, without leaving any projecting ftraws; which, when not cut or finged away, (as fhould always be done when the hives are rough,) would occafion much unneceffary trouble to the bees, when put into them, to gnaw them off. When the hives are made, and, if neceffary, gently finged with ftraw, four fmall fticks fhould be fixed acrofs the infide of them, at proper diftances, in order not only to keep the hive firm, but alfo to prevent the combs from falling down, (which they would otherwife do by their own weight;) or from being fhifted out of their places, when the hives are rapped upon, or difturbed accidentally.

Some ingenious gentlemen have made their hives to confift of different apartments, though inhabited only by one fwarm. This kind of hives are called COLONIES; but I do not much approve of them; as the partitions prevent that accumulation of heat, which is neceffary for

for the health of the whole family; and as
fome of the rooms muft be colder than others,
the bees, efpecially in winter, will all draw to
one place; leaving the other apartments empty,
and expofed to fuch a degree of cold, as will
probably make the honey candy and become
ufelefs. Befides this method is unnatural, for the
bees always lodge in one apartment, when left
to their own liberty, provided it be large e-
nough to hold them: and as they lay their
eggs in the middle part of their combs and
hives firft, and afterwards gradually enlarge
the brood around the centre of the hive, they
not only get them more eafily defended from
all danger, but alfo fooner hatched, by the fuperior degree of heat.

Colonies have never yet been, and I am perfuaded never will be extended to general ufe,
although it is nearly two centuries fince they
were invented by JOHN GEDDY, Efq. I will
not deny, however, that bees may thrive pretty well upon this plan; which muft be allowed to have one advantage, as, when properly
conftructed, thefe hives afford an opportunity
to the inquifitive philofopher of feeing the bees
carry on their labours. Colony hives are made
in various forms, according to the tafte of

T 2   different

different gentlemen. Some confift of three boxes, placed one above another; others of an equal number placed collaterally; and a third kind are made with one box in the front, another behind that, and the third behind the fecond. All thefe different kinds have fquare holes in the fides or tops of the boxes, to allow the bees liberty to go from one box to another, as they may find neceffary; and there are fmall panes of glafs fixed in them, in order to obferve the operations of the bees; with wooden fhutters to cover the glafs, when it is not intended to infpect the hive.

I have feen, in thofe favourable years when the bees had fwarmed very liberally, that the proprietors have been greatly diftreffed for want of hives, to receive their fecond and fubfequent fwarms. But an experienced beemafter will never be at a lofs in fuch circumftances. If all his empty hives are filled, and if he intends to take honey in Autumn, he will find many other articles in which they will chearfully build and work; fuch as any large jar, half barrel, tub, pot, or box of any kind, that is large enough. For the bees are not delicate in their choice of a habitation; witnefs the well known inftance of SAMSON's dead lion.

lon. They will work in any place during Summer; for although the manufacture of honey and honey combs is ſo natural to them, that they can work at no other employment, yet the *ſhop* in which they make them, is a matter of indifference to them, provided it is only large enough, and capable of excluding cold, rain and robbers. Even darkneſs itſelf is no diſparagement, but rather renders their habitation more agreeable to them.

C H A P. XIX.

OF THE NATURAL SWARMING OF BEES.

As it would evidence a conſiderable degree of folly to deſert an old beaten path, for a new road, unleſs the latter were both nearer and better, ſo I would by no means recommend artificial ſwarming, if natural ſwarms can be obtained. But even, in the latter caſe, many uſeful directions may be given, and ſhall be laid down in as plain a manner as poſſible.

We

We fhall likewife fhow, how it is fometimes e-
qually neceffary and advantageous to make artificial fwarms, along with the manner of doing it to the beft advantage, when it is neceffary.

As the time when a hive will throw a
fwarm is quite uncertain, efpecially to young
beginners in the bee-hufbandry, a conftant attendance is neceffary in fwarming time, from
eight o'clock in the morning till about three
or four in the afternoon. But this may be
done with little trouble or expence. A boy,
or a girl, or any old perfon, may be employed
to watch the bees during thefe hours; and this
needs only to be done in fine days, as the bees
feldom fend out a colony in cold, damp, or
chilly weather.

Some hives will ly out long before they fwarm,
though they will fwarm at laft; others, although
they lie out equally long, will not fwarm at
all; a third clafs will fwarm without the fmalleft previous appearance; and a fourth will
make a buftle about their doors, for three or
four days before they fwarm: And, therefore,
from fuch a variety of chances, it is fcarce poffible to determine the precife time of fwarming; although we may reafonably conjecture,
from

from the following fymptoms, that this wifhed for period is approaching.

When the number of bees in a hive increafes faft, about the end of May and beginning of June, and drones appear among them ; if a fhort time before this, water of an infipid tafte appeared on the ftool, about or within the entry ; if this water, which is called *fweat*, and is occafioned by the increafed heat of the hive, be dried up, by the ftill greater increafe of that heat, from the bees becoming more and more numerous ; if the bees, about 11 o'clock, A. M. fly about in a reeling manner, making a noife and motion about the front of the hive ; all thefe are figns to put the Bee-mafter on his guard, and to prepare him for the joyful event that is faft approaching, of a young colony within a day or two, or even, perhaps, within an hour or two. But if the bees, after all this, run haftily up and down the outfide of the hive, and at laft gather together in a clufter upon the ftool, he may call his friends together, to behold his increafing ftore, as he may depend that they will fwarm immediately : * and nothing can furely be more delightful

* It is indeed furprizing, to fee the young colony leaving their mother

to the bee-mafter, than to behold the young emigrants flying in the air and darkening the fky with a thoufand varying lines.

Mean-time, while he is fatisfying his curio-fity as to the manner of their fwarming, he fhould obferve, whether they are beginning to fettle upon any place, in, or near his own apia-ry,

hive, and deferting it feemingly in the utmoft hurry and precipi-tation, in fo much that they can hardly clear the way for each other. A ftranger to the nature of thefe wonderful infects would be apt to conclude, that there was fome formidable ene-my within, who was murdering them by wholefale, and from whom they were flying for their lives; or elfe that they were leaving a difagreeable habitation, where there was nothing but war and poverty; and emigrating to fome happier fituation, where they would enjoy peace and plenty. But the reverfe of all this is the truth; for they are going away of their own ac-cord, chearfully parting with their deareft friends, and leaving a warm habitation, and well-ftored granary, to feek their fortunes in a new fituation, where they will have every thing to provide for themfelves, and all the varieties and inconftancy of weather and climate to ftruggle againft.

An old cuftom ftill prevails with many, when a fwarm of bees are rifing, to make a tinkling noife upon a pan, or kettle, as they think that the noife makes them fettle the fooner, and prevents them from flying away. But I am of opinion, that when the fwarm comes naturally off, it is proper that they fhould hear and underftand each other, which a noife of this kind will prevent. On all fuch occafions therefore, I ufe none. But, when the bees attempt to fly off, all kinds of noife fhould then be ufed, to fright-en and prevent them from hearing each other, and thus incline them to fettle at home.

ry, or attempting to fly away, which they
they will fometimes do. If the former, he
fhould keep at a diftance till they fettle, as going near them might not only prevent them
from fettling, but might alfo occafion the death
of fome of them, by trampling upon them.

As foon as they alight on any thing, that can
eafily be brought to the ground, fuch as the
fmall branch of a tree, or a berry bufh, or the
like, let a fheet be fpread on the ground near
the fwarm, and two fticks placed upon it, a foot
afunder. Then place the fwarm upon the fheet,
between the fticks, and gently cover it with a
hive †, refting the edges of the hive upon the
fticks, to prevent it from crufhing any of the
bees ; who will thus have free air, and accefs to
and from the hive, which muft be covered with
a cloth, to prevent the rays of the fun from
fcorching the bees, and provoking them to rife
and feek out a more comfortable habitation. If
their new lodging pleafes them, they will take

U immediate

---

† Some advife to rub the hive, before it be placed over the
fwarm, with a little honey, or fugar and ale mixed, in order to
allure the bees. This can do no harm, but I feldom adopt the
practice, as I have feen little or no benefit from it ; the Queen
getting into the hive is the only allurement to excite the bees to
go into it, and alfo to keep them there, when they are gone fafely in.

immediate poffeffion, and fall to work with alacrity. Sometimes, after continuing two or three
hours in it, and beginning to work, they will
rife and fettle on fome other place, or go back
to their mother hive again; and fometimes they
will fly off altogether, in fearch perhaps of a
habitation previoufly fixed on. They muft
therefore be carefully watched till the heat of
the day be over, after which, it may be prefumed, they will not rife again.

As foon as the young colony are fairly lodged
in their new habitation, let the hive be placed
on a ftool, and carried with all due caution to
the place where it is intended to ftand ‡; for
the fooner the hive is ftationed, the fooner the
bees will be acquainted with its fituation. A
few ftragglers, indeed, may fly about the place
where the fheet was firft laid down; but they
will foon either find out the fwarm, or return
to their mother hive, either of which will be no
lofs. When the hive is placed in its proper
ftation

‡ At all feafons, as foon as a fwarm is fairly fettled, both the
fize of the fwarm and the feafon of the year fhould be taken into
confideration. If the fwarm be pretty numerous, if the mother
hive can bear the want of it, and if the feafon be not too far advanced, let it be put into a hive by itfelf. But directions will
afterwards be given, how to act if any of the contrary circumftances occur.

ftation, the cloth fhould be allowed to remain
upon it, to keep off the rays of the fun §, till
night, when the fkirts may be plaftered over
with lime mixed with hair, and thus fixed to
the ftool, and the top covered with turf, as formerly directed, page 97.

Sometimes, though feldom, a fwarm will
fly off, notwithftanding every method that can
be ufed to prevent it. This happens only in
very fine calm weather, when the bees have

U 2 had

---

§ Sometimes, in very hot weather, young fwarms have fuffered
greatly, by the intenfe heat melting the wax, and making their
combs fall down on the ftool, in confequence of which the honey
runs out, the bees are befmeared, the young ones bruifed, and
the hive almoft totally ruined. Many hives fuffered in this manner, by the great heat laft fummer, (1794;) but fuch misfortunes
only happen in the beft years for honey ; and, indeed, it is to be
regretted, that we have fo feldom reafon to complain of too much
heat.

In fuch favourable years, the beft method to prevent fuch confequences, is to keep the young fwarms, (for the ftock hives are
in no danger,) well fcreened from the fcorching rays of the fun,
by covering them over on the fouth fide, or placing fcreens before the hives in fuch a manner as to keep off the heat, at the
fame time, that they do not obftruct the bees from going out and
in to their work. One of the large boards or ftools, which the
hives ufually ftand on, being placed on edge upon the ftool before the entry to the hive, but in fuch a pofition that the bees
may have free accefs and egrefs, will anfwer this purpofe, and
can eafily be removed, as foon as the exceffive heat is over.

had liberty some days before fwarming, to
roam about in fearch of a commodious habitation; which, if once they find, it is difficult,
and often impoffible, to prevent them from e-
migrating to it. When the weather is very
favourable, the bees often, before fwarming,
fend out fcouts in fearch of a proper habitation; and when they difcover a hive whofe
bees are dead, or any empty place about the
roof of a gentleman's houfe, or a church, caftle, or trunk of a tree ; more efpecially, if bees
have wrought combs in it the fummer before,
but have died out of it in winter, they will
fend out a fquadron of bees, three or four days
before they fwarm, to clean out the place, and
render it fit for the reception of the young colony, the firft favourable opportunity. At
fuch places, I have often feen a confiderable
number of bees, bufily employed in clearing
away the dead bees, broken crumbs of wax,
and all other rubbifh; and fometimes I have obferved bees from different hives, laying an equal
claim to the newly difcovered habitation, and,
as mankind too often do in fimilar cafes, fighting and killing each other for the uninhabited
territory ; for, two fwarms have been feen flying

ing to fuch a place in one day, in which cafe
a bloody battle between them often becomes
inevitable.

There have been many inftances of a fwarm
of bees flying in a direct line to a dead hive,
when it happened to be within their reach in
a neighbouring apiary. Such hives are often
left ftanding by the owner, either from his
not knowing that the bees are dead, or from
his ignorance of the confequences. They are
alfo frequently left by roguifh bee-mafters, on
purpofe to entice their neighbours fwarms;
which is as villainous as ftealing a fwarm, if
not more fo. Mr Maxwell fays, there is a law
againft fuffering a dead hive to ftand in an
apiary. If there is, it is a very juft one, but
if not, an act of parliament fhould be paffed
againft fuch a pernicious practice. Such
caufes have been feveral times tried in courts
of juftice, and fome judges have punifhed the
trefpafs, which was certainly juft. But I lately heard of a caufe of this nature, which was
tried before a judge, who affoilzied the aggref-
for, upon this principle, that every man has
a right to keep what he pleafes in his own garden. By this decifion the judge evidenced his
ignorance ; for, if fuch a precedent were
once

once eftablifhed as law, no perfon, who has
a covetous bee-mafter in his neighbourhood,
would be fure to lofe fome fwarms of his bees;
for, a dead hive, left ftanding in an apiary
during fummer, feldom fails to receive a fwarm
before Lammas.

Many have been not a little difficulted how
to determine, whether the old hive that the
fwarm went into, had living bees in it or not,
before that event took place. One eafy method of deciding this point, is, by infpecting
it, to fee if there are live young in it; and
another is, by the diftance from which the
fwarm has come; for, I know for certain, that
a fwarm will not fly a mile to a living hive;
whereas, they will fly four miles to take poffeffion of an old one with combs in it, whofe inhabitants are dead. I have, indeed, feen a fwarm go
into a living hive, that ftood in the fame apiary;
but this was rather accidental than otherwife.
The Queen returning home in confufion, perhaps from a fruitlefs expedition, might miftake another hive for her own. In fuch cafes,
a great battle frequently enfues, in which many are flain, and often the Queen among them.
Sometimes I have feen them agree very well,
and make a good colony, when the hive was

properly

properly raifed with a very large eek. At o-
ther times, I have feen a fwarm, after joining
another hive, being well received, and remaining in it very peaceably, come off, notwithftanding, the very next day.

When a fwarm emigrates, with a view to fettle in fome habitation, which their fpies had
previoufly difcovered, they fly to the place in a
direct line. The bee-mafter fhould, therefore,
run or ride along with them, as far as he can ;
for on fuch occafions they fometimes fly fo flow,
as a perfon who is fwift of foot may accompany
them. But if he fhould be prevented from following them in a direct line, by any interruptions
from woods, waters, or inclofures, let him, upon
recovering the line, proceed ftraight forward,
without turning to the right or left, and the
chance is ten to one that he will difcover them,
efpecially if they happen to alight or reft upon
any dike hedge, or brufh by the way. But
fhould this not happen, upon proceeding ftill
forward, the line will probably lead him to
fome garden where there is an apiary ; the
owner of which fhould be told the cafe ; and
if he is an honeft man, he will doubtlefs allow
his hives to be fearched, in the prefence of wit-
neffes, to fee if the fwarm have taken up their
abode

abode in any of his dead hives. This will eafily be difcovered by examining the entries of his hives, and if there are any fmall crumbs of wax lying like as much faw duft, on the ftool before them, it may be prefumed, that the bees of the new fwarm have cleaned it off the combs; and, therefore, a farther fearch fhould be demanded; and upon turning up the hive, and fearching with a fmall ftick for young bees in the cells, as directed, (p. 120) the matter can foon be decided, whether the hive was inhabited by living bees, previous to the fwarm entering it, or not. If fealed up maggots, or young bees appear in the cells, the owner of the fwarm can have no claim; but if none of thefe appear, he has a right to the hive, which, if the proprietor of the apiary fhould refufe to deliver, he ought to be inftantly fummoned before a Magiftrate, while the hive is ftill totally deficient of young bees; when the cafe being plainly ftated, and *this decifive proof* adduced, the young fwarm will doubtlefs be ordered to be reftored, and the greedy proprietor of the dead hive in all probability fined for his covetoufnefs.

But if the fwarm fhould not have alighted at the firft apiary in the direct line, the owner fhould ftill proceed ftraight forward, and he

will

will in all probability arrive at another apiary,
where the fame inquiries and mode of inveftigation fhould be repeated : Or if any hollow
tree, church, gentleman's manfion-houfe, old
ruin, or any other building, fhould happen to
lie in the direct line, they fhould be infpected
attentively, and proper inquiries made at the
people in the neighbourhood, if they obferved
a fwarm of bees flying or fettling on any of
them. By thefe means perfevered in, a difco-
very will certainly be made ; and if the fwarm
has fettled in any fuch place, the following directions will fhow the method of taking them
out in this and other cafes of a like nature. If
a fwarm fettle in a hollow tree, or any cavity of a building, it will be impoffible to get it
out by any other means, than taking them out
by handfuls. Some indeed, alledge, that rapping will force them out ; but not one fwarm
of twenty will yield to that method, unlefs the
Queen can be laid hold of, and brought out.
The owner fhould, therefore, make as much
room as poffible, to get his hand introduced, fo
as to pull them out by handfuls, and put them
into an empty hive ; and as foon as he is fo fortunate as to get hold of the Queen, he fhould
put her into the hive, where fhe will prevent

X   '   the

the bees from ftraying; and thofe that were ftill remaining in the building or hollow tree, will quickly come to the hive, and join the reft. In fuch cafes, I have fearched whole hours for the Queen, who generally hides herfelf with fo much art, that it is extremely difficult to lay hold of her, although in fuch fearches I feldom failed to catch her at laft. But when the Queen cannot, by any means, be got, and when all or the greateft part of the fwarm is recovered, let the hole be clofe fhut up, and a weak hive brought, and re-inforced with the common bees, (as directed page 142) which is the beft ufe that can be made of them in fuch cafes.

Before bees fwarm the fecond or third time, they do not ly out in clufters about the hive or upon the ftool; but as foon as they are ready, they come off in a body, even in weather that is by no means favourable. The figns, when thefe after fwarms will come off, are more certain than thofe that precede the firft fwarming; for, if the weather be good, one may almoft prognofticate the very hour. By liftening at night to the found of a hive, about eight, ten, or twelve days, after the firft fwarm is gone off, that peculiar found, commonly called *tolling*, will be eafily diftinguifhed. This found

feems

feems to be the royal proclamation iffued by the young princefs, to warn, or rather to invite her fellow emigrants to prepare for their intended journey. It founds, fays one, as if the words *peep! peep! peep!* were rapidly pronounced fifteen or twenty times in half a minute. She then ftops, and begins again repeatedly, like a chicken peeping for its mother, when it has loft her. When there are feveral young Queens in the hive, there will be fo many diftinct voices repeating this call. I have fometimes heard thefe princeffes calling from all corners of the hive ; and, as it were, anfwering each other ; fome calling out *peep, peep,* in a treble voice, and others anfwering in a voice rather more hoarfe, and comparatively like bafs *. When thefe founds are heard

X 2

in

---

* Almoft all authors agree, that thefe peculiar voices proceed from the young Queens *petitioning* (fo to fpeak,) for *leave* to emigrate with a young fwarm. I have fometimes thought, however, that this noife might alfo proceed from fear or rage being excited amongft them. I was led to entertain this opinion, by obferving their different fcreams one day, which made me fufpect that there were more than one Queen in the hive. And as I wifhed to have one or two of them to enable me to caufe fome out-laying hives fwarm, I drove all the bees out of that hive. One Queen went along with them ; but I ftill perceived other two Queens, befides three royal cells fealed up. I ftill heard the ufual quick cry of the Queen ; and, upon attentively obferving their motions;

in the hive, the emigration of a fwarm may be depended upon, within a day or two at moft, if the weather holds tolerably good. The firft night that thefe founds are obfervable, they are low, and not very frequent, nor even the next day ; but, on the fecond night, they become louder and more frequent, in fo much that they may fometimes be diftinguifhed at the diftance of fome yards from the hive. Next day, if the weather be favourable, a fwarm may be depended upon. " It is delightful, (fays Mr THORLEY) to hear thofe peculiar and " mufical founds or notes, being an eight or " chord, which is truly harmonious." They are fcarcely ever heard before a firft fwarm goes off; I believe not once in fixty cafes. The reafon, I fuppofe, is, that they have in general, only one Queen reared to go off with the firft fwarm ; and fometimes, when tempted by very fine weather, even the old Queen will go off with the firft colony, before the

young

tions, I faw them going to the royal cells, and tear at them with great fury, fcreaming and roaring feemingly with great indignation :—a phænomenon, which I could only account for, upon the principle of their entertaining a jealoufy left their rivals in the cell fhould come forward, and ftand in competitition with them

young princefs comes out of the royal cell. *
Whereas, before the fecond or third emigration takes place, they will fometimes have two
or three Queens, and as many royal cells, in
their hive; one of which may be taken to fupply any hive that needs them.

Often have I feen a young Queen take an
airing. For inftance, in Summer 1790, I had
a hive that had no Queen in it, but a pregnant
royal cell, which had been feven days fealed
up; on which account, I expected that a
Queen

---

* The Queens are generally bred in fwarming time, as may
be obferved by turning up a hive at that period, when the royal
cells may be perceived on the edges or fides of the combs, although fometimes they hang from the middle. Thefe cells are
of an oblong circular form, of confiderable thicknefs, and in appearance rather clumfy. One of them will weigh as much as
four or five fcore of common cells. When half made, they are
not unlike the lower part of an acorn, turned upfide down; they
gradually lengthen, and, when finifhed and fcaled up, are about
an inch in length, and would refemble the end of one's little
finger, if it wanted the nail. In fwarming time, there will fometimes be from one to fix of thefe royal cells; though commonly
there are not above two or three. They all hang perpendicu-
larly, with their open ends pointing downwards to the ftool.
After the young Queens are hatched, thefe cells are fometimes
removed by the bees, and fometimes allowed to remain; but I never faw an egg laid in an old cell to be a Queen; for the bees
always build a new cell when they want a young Queen.

Queen would foon emerge out of the cell. And, as I was anxious to fee what appearance fhe made the moment of her birth, I turned up the hive every hour, and luckily hit the time that fhe was opening the cell for herfelf, when I faw her come out of it, and creep a-bout pretty well. Two days thereafter, I faw her come to the entry of the hive, and fly off and take an airing. She returned within a-bout ten minutes thereafter, and went back in-to the hive, where the bees received her with joy. I have alfo feen many other young Queens do the fame on the fecond or third day of their age. Perhaps old ones may do fo too; but I think this happens very feldom, as they are large and heavy, and confequently may be afraid to truft themfelves to their wings. No doubt, the old Queens can fly when they pleafe, although, like many old people, they are not very fond of much travel.

It will fometimes happen, in an apiary where there is a confiderable number of bee-hives, that two fwarms will go together in the time of fwarming, when they chance to come out of their mother hives nearly about the fame time. When one fwarm is nearly fettled on a bufh, hedge, or any other place, and another begins

to

to come off from the mother hive, the mufic of the former invites the latter to join them. In fuch circumftances, therefore, the moft effectual method to prevent the junction of the two fwarms, is to cover the firft fwarm completely with a large fheet, which will prevent the other fwarm from hearing their melody. But if the firft fwarm be got into a hive, or nearly all entered, it fhould be carried into a houfe, and kept there for fome little time, till the fecond fwarm be fairly fettled fomewhere; after which the hive fhould be brought back to its former fituation. But when both fwarms are fmall, or but of a medium fize, if they unite voluntarily and peaceably together, as they generally do in fuch cafes, their junction will be rather an advantage than a lofs: For it is certain, that 16,000 bees in one hive will collect more honey and wax than the fame number of bees lodged in two different hives could poffibly do*.

CHAP.

* This can be eafily accounted for. In every hive there is a certain number of bees appointed to hatch the young, and to defend the hive from robbers, &c. Now, fuppofing that each hive requires 2,000 bees to be daily occupied in thefe employments, then it follows, that 16,000 bees, lodged in two different hives, muft devote 4,000 of their number to thefe objects, and

leave

CHAP. XXI.

OF THE ARTIFICIAL SWARMING OF BEES.

ALTHOUGH, in moſt caſes, bees are beſt directed by natural inſtinct, and on that account
I

leave only 12,000 at work in both hives, whereas, the ſame number of bees in ONE hive, requiring only 2,000 to be devoted to theſe employments, will allow 14,000 to be conſtantly employed in the fields, and of courſe one ſeventh part more honey and wax may be produced in the courſe of the ſeaſon. There are alſo other advantages ariſing from ſuch a junction of ſmall ſwarms: They require, for inſtance, only one place in the garden; being more in number; they afford more heat to bring forward the young, and they are more able to defend the hive from robbers, &c. &c.

And here it may be both uſeful and entertaining, to take notice of the various weights and numbers of different ſwarms. " It " has been found, (ſays BUTLER,) that a larger number than " 40 or 50,000 will not thrive together in one hive. Swarms " often amount to 30,000; a large ſwarm may weigh eight " pounds, and gradually leſs to one pound; conſequently a " very good one weighs five or ſix pounds, a moderate one " four pounds. No ſwarms leſs than this ſhould be kept, but " united with others." If we conſider that about 5000 bees weigh a pound, a ſwarm weighing four pounds, will have near about 20,000 bees, which will compoſe a very good ſwarm. But I am of opinion, that a ſwarm, conſiſting of 15,000 bees, will do very well in a ſingle hive, if the ſeaſon is not too far advanced; and, indeed, the more numerous the ſwarm is, ſo much the better. I myſelf have had above 30,000 bees in one ſwarm.

I am always beft pleafed with natural fwarms, yet it may be obferved of them, as well as of moft other animals, intended for the ufe or benefit of man, that confiderable room is left for human art and ingenuity to affift them. Thus, for inftance, they are provided by human art with much more convenient habitations, than they could either rear or difcover by their own inftinct: For, without our aid, if no ruinous houfe or hollow tree were near, a young fwarm might hang on a bufh, till they were either totally deftroyed by wind, or drowned by rain. Artificial fwarming, therefore, when a natural fwarm (which is always preferable,) cannot be obtained, is fometimes a neceffary and ufeful part of bee hufbandry; and will, indeed, turn out ultimately to our own advantage, as will appear from what follows.

Before proceeding farther, however, with any directions on this fubject, it is proper to caution the reader, that although artificial fwarming is very profitable, when properly performed by an experienced bee-mafter, yet it always has been, and ever will be, very deftructive to bees, if performed by unfkilful perfons: and, indeed, all new beginners may

Y

be

be almoſt certain of ruining ſome hives in their firſt attempts. But, by carefully obſerving the following directions, the moſt inexperienced bee-maſter may ſoon come to the practical knowledge of the art, and thereby avoid ſuch blunders as would prove deſtructive to his bees.

CASE I. Sometimes, when two ſwarms meet, a dreadful battle enſues, on account of there being two Queens among them. Each party ſeems determined to defend their own Queen and mother at the riſk of their lives. Their fury generally laſts till one of the Queens is ſlain, after which a peace commonly takes place, and the two bands unite harmoniouſly in one community*.

But

---

* In theſe conflicts, it is aſtoniſhing to ſee what dreadful havock they make in a very ſhort time. In my younger years, I have ſeen above 1000 of theſe brave winged ſoldiers lying weltering in their gore, within the ſpace of ten minutes. The Queen of one or both ſwarms is often ſeized inſtantaneouſly, and murdered. On ſuch occaſions, I have ſeen above an hundred bees, all wrapt together in a cluſter, of the ſize of a ſmall apple, and ſo firmly compacted together around the body of a Queen, that it was with the utmoſt difficulty I could ſeparate them from her. Moſt writers are of opinion, that the bees, which thus cluſter round a Queen, are her enemies, and that their being ſo cloſely compacted together about her proceeds from the keen enmity

of

But, if they do not unite in a friendly manner, there is not a moment to be loft. The
hive muft be inftantly turned up, and the bees
driven into four or five different hives. Every
clufter of them muft be fearched for the
Queen, who, when caught, muft be feparated from all the other bees, whether friends or
foes, as, at fuch a time, it is impoffible to diftinguifh the one from the other. And, while
fhe is kept clofe prifoner, the bees may be
frightened from farther fighting; and even
gradually pacified, by rapping on the hives,
and thus driven out of one hive into another.
If this attempt does not fucceed to bring the
bees to a good underftanding with each other;
cold water may be fprinkled on them in the
hives to cool their courage; or they may be
taken into a room, as directed, page 142, and
when, by their being thus toffed and tumbled
about, (all due care being taken, however, not

Y 2

to

of each to be firft at her with his dagger. It is, indeed, beyond
a doubt, that Queens are often furrounded in this manner by
their enemies, who frequently kill them very quickly. But I
am of opinion, that they are often likewife encompaffed by their
friends in a fimilar manner, whofe loyal zeal for their fovereign
mother leads them thus to form an impregnable phalanx around
her with their bodies, to protect her perfon from the rage of her
moft inveterate foes.

to hurt them) their spirits are brought low, they may be put into two different hives, and a Queen offered to each. To try their temper, however, a specimen of the bees may be first introduced to the Queen, and if they treat her with mildnefs, she may then be introduced to the whole swarm. But, if they appear to be still in bad humour, the Queen should be kept back till they become more pacific, which they will quickly do; for as soon as they get leifr e to think, they will mifs their Queen, and make all poffible enquiry after her, running up and down the hive with the utmost impatience and anxiety, in search of their sovereign mother; and, when they cannot discover her any where, they will conclude that she has perished during the tumult, and most of them will creep out of the hive in defpair, and crawl about on the ground till they die; their cafe being quite defperate, as they have not an egg to raife another Queen from. Some will perhaps attempt to fly home, hoping to find their mother there; and others will try if they can gain admittance into any other hive. This is the critical moment to prefent a Queen to them. As foon as a few of them difcover her, they will furround her with the greatest

pleafure

pleafure, and fing aloud for joy. The reft, hearing the joyful news, will all crowd around her, and be ready to fuffocate her in their extacy. She fhould then be placed on the ftool, as in other cafes ; but if, during the conflict, one or both Queens have been killed, the bees may either be reftored to their original hives, or put into any others where they fhall be moft favourably received.

In this laft fpring, (1795,) having two hives, that had but few bees in each, I put the bees of the one hive into the other ; fufpecting, that as they had both bred flowly, there might be a defect in the health of one or both of their Queens ; and hoping that, by putting them together, the bees would probably hold a confultation, which of the two Queens was moft healthy, and, after electing her, kill or banifh the other, as they thought proper. The common bees of both hives at once united kindly and feemed happy ; but, upon turning up the hive within 20 minutes after, to fee if all was well, I perceived a few bees cluftered together, which, however, did not greatly furprife me, as I thought the conjoined republics had already decided, which Queen fhould remain in the hive, and that thefe bees were leading the rejected

rejected Queen to exile or execution. But, u-
pon a more clofe infpection, I obferved the two
Queens ftruggling together with the utmoft
fury, and darting the moft deadly blows at each
other. Being afraid of lofing both, and thereby
ruining the united hive, by their mutually killing each other, which muft have been the
cafe, had one of them thruft her fting into the
other's body and left it, as fometimes happens,
though rarely *, among the common bees in
fuch conflicts, I feparated them, and kept them
afunder, though they ftill ran with great fury
in fearch of each other along the table §. I then
took

---

* Inftances of this do not happen above once, perhaps, in fifty
times ; although the fact is certain, that they fometimes kill
themfelves, by leaving their ftings in the bodies of their oppon-
ents.

§ The above-mentioned battle, between the two Queen
Bees, reminded me, at the time, of thofe lines in the old fong
of Chevy-Chace ; where the brave DOUGLAS is reprefented as
faying,

    " But truft me, PIERCY, pity it were,
      " And great offence to kill
    " Any of thefe, our harmlefs men,
      " For they have done no ill.

    " Let you and I, the battle try,
      " And fet our men afide,"
    " Then c—ft be he, (quoth Earl PIERCY,)
      " By whom it is denied."

took the one that appeared to be the boldeſt, and put her again into the hive, where ſhe was kindly received by the bees, and put the other Queen into another hive, to be dealt with, as the bees might incline, as I had no other uſe for her at that ſeaſon.

Let not my readers, from this account, ſuppoſe, that the common bees are a race of cowards, who will ſtand regardleſs and indifferent, while their ſovereigns or mothers are in danger. On the contrary, they are a ſet of brave and *patriotic* warriors, who will riſk their lives in defence of their hive, their property, or their ſovereign mother. But, when a *duel* takes place between two Queen bees, they commonly, nay almoſt always, diſpatch one of the Queens themſelves.

CASE II. If the rays of the ſun have been intercepted by a cloud, or a ſhower of rain has occurred in the time of ſwarming, the ſmallneſs of the ſwarm may be aſcribed to theſe circumſtances having prevented the half of the young colony from leaving the mother hive. In this caſe, let the ſwarm be placed where the original hive ſtood, for about a quarter of an hour, in which time, the bees that are returning from the fields, will ſoon make the

ſwarm

fwarm large enough, and then the fwarm fhould be removed to about a mile diftance, to prevent the bees from going back to the old ftock again.*

CASE III. When a perfon has a fmall fwarm, whether it be a firft, fecond or third one, and at the fame time a lying-out hive, that has been long in fwarming, he fhould drive all the bees out of the lying-out hive, into an empty one, (fee the method, page 138) and fet down the bees in the fame fpot where they ftood formerly, which will make a fine large artificial fwarm, as fuch a hive would have abundance of bees; after which, let the fmall fwarm be put into the old hive, where they will hatch out all the young, and make a good hive; and let the old hive be placed on the fame fpot where the fmall fwarm ftood.

CASE

* When bees come naturally off in a fwarm, they take a view of the place where they fettle, and never think of going back to their mother hive; but, when they are feparated from their mother hive by driving, or when the hive is fhifted from where it formerly ftood, they are infenfible of the change of their fituation, and always fly back to their former ftation; for which reafon, the bee-mafter fhould always remove every artificial fwarm, or re-inforced hive, to fome confiderable diftance, otherwife a number of the bees will go back again.

CASE IV. If there are two fmall fwarms, but no hives, that have bees fufficient either to exchange with, or re-inforce them, let them be united; for, in fuch cafes, two fwarms, con-joined into one, will profper better, and turn out more profitable, than three fmall ones kept feparate. See page 167.

CASE V. Suppofe one drive all the bees out of a hive, and thereby make an artificial fwarm, if the old hive has a royal cell in it, by introducing about 5000 common bees into it, they will hatch out the young Queen, with all the eggs and nymphs (or young bees) in the cells, and render it a flourifhing hive. The method of introducing the common bees, is as follows: Let a ftrong lying-out hive be removed from its ufual fituation, about 10 A. M. and place the hive that has no bees on the fpot where it ftood. The bees, on their return from the fields, will enter it, and will no doubt be furprized at the fudden revolution, having left their hive full of their brethren, not one of whom is now to be feen; but, finding plenty of honey, and abundance of eggs, they will make the beft of their mis-fortune, and fpeedily replenifh the hive, by rearing up the young bees, and working with as much alacrity, if not more, than when they

Z   were

were in their original hive. It will be necessary, however, in this operation, to remove the original hive to another apiary, (See p. 176.)

CASE VI. When one has a hive that has long lien out, and still shows no appearance of swarming, if a swarm is wished for, all the bees may be driven out, as directed, page 138. A swarm may thus be obtained, which, if the weather answers, will not fail to succeed. The old hive may be placed below some other hive, the bees whereof will hatch out the young bees, and in autumn the honey may be taken out of it, and all the bees put into the upper hive.

CASE VII. I have often formerly taken all the bees out of a hive to make an artificial swarm, and put into it a considerable number of common bees, in order to hatch out the young brood in the combs, build a royal cell, and rear a Queen for themselves. This practice I found in general answered very well, as the bees hardly ever failed to rear a Queen. The only objection against it arises from this consideration, that from the time the old Queen is taken away, till the young one is fit to lay eggs, a period of twenty five days elapses, during which time there is not a single egg laid in the hive. And when it is farther considered, that there

muft

muſt be an additional loſs of other 18 days, before the eggs can be bees for any uſe, it is evident, that the beſt part of the honey ſeaſon will be over, and conſequently that by autumn, the hive will be greatly deficient in bees. For theſe reaſons I have now almoſt entirely given up the practice, though I have ſometimes had hives that proſpered very well under it. And, indeed, if I intended to kill a hive of bees in autumn, I would rather prefer the taking away their Queen from them about the end of July, and leaving a great number of common bees in the hive, which, as they would have few bees to nurſe up, would collect a greater quantity of honey in that period, than if they had a Queen in the hive daily laying eggs for them, which would employ a good number of the bees, both to hatch and nurſe up the young, and the re-by, the fewer would be employed in collecting honey.

CASE VIII. If a ſwarm ſhould come off, which the mother hive cannot afford to want without great injury, it ought to be returned again into the old hive, in this manner : Take the Queen from the new ſwarm and confine her in a box ; and then turn up the hive containing the new ſwarm, and place it before the entry of the old

ſtock

ftock which the bees came from, in fuch a manner that the bees in it may run from it into the
entry of the old hive again ; which they will
foon cheerfully do, efpecially as their Queen was
taken from them.   This operation is fo eafy
that it may almoft be performed by a child.

CASE IX. When the fummer is far advanced, and it may be rather late for fwarming, an
eek, placed below a ftrong hive, will give the
bees more room to work, and may prevent a
late fwarm from coming off, which, in general,
turns out more lofs than advantage to the Bee-
mafter.

CHAP. XXII.

OF THE KILLING OF DRONES.

IT is a good fign that a hive is thriving, and
a certain proof that there is a Queen in it, when
the working bees kill their drones early : for
in thofe hives that have loft their Queen, the
bees become fo carelefs both about their honey
and

and their hive, that they permit the drones to
live till November or December. And perhaps
there is no fmall wifdom in this, for the bees,
knowing that they cannot breed any more, are
probably fenfible, that they will gain more by
the additional heat of the drones preferving
them from the feverity of the winter, than they
will lofe by the expence of maintaining them ;
and confequently lengthen out their own lives,
as well as thofe of the drones.

This leads me to think, that the drones are
not fo fhort-lived as is generally believed. If
the working bees did not kill them in the end
of fummer and beginning of harveft, but left
them to die of old age, they might perhaps live
in a good warm hive till fpring. The bees feldom begin to kill the drones, till the honey feafon be nearly over. When, therefore, the maf-
facre of the drones begins, one may know that,
in general, the honey is becoming rather fcarce
in their neighbourhood; although it is not an infallible fign ; for the bees of fome hives kill their
drones fooner than thofe of others, ftanding in
the fame apiary. In hives fituated near early
paftures, when the flowers are moftly gone,
the bees will kill their drones in the end of
July. In later fituations, they are permited to
live

live till Auguſt. During this laſt autumn,
(1794,) I ſaw many excellent thriving hives,
ſituated among good heath, whoſe drones were
not extirpated till about the end of September.

As the working bees, when the flowers become ſcarce, kill the drones, and thus ſhow us
plainly, that they are now become uſeleſs in
the hive ; ſo I agree with almoſt every writer
on this ſubject, that it is proper to aſſiſt the
bees in extirpating them. The manner in
which the working bees kill the drones is this.
They not only ſting them, but pull and bite
them with their teeth. It is incredible what
havock they will make of them in a ſingle
day, as I have often been convinced, by obſerving great numbers of them lying dead before the door of the hive ‡. They alſo ſometimes

‡ When the bees once fall a-killing the drones, it is amazing
to ſee how intent they are on the buſineſs.—They not only
diſpatch the old ones, but they alſo tear out and deſtroy the
young drone-maggots in the cells,—eſpecially in bad weather.
I have indeed ſeen them, even before ſwarming time, when it
had been wet weather for five or ſix days, become ſo diſconſolate,
ſo diſcouraged, and even deſperate, (thinking, perhaps, that the
weather would never mend,) that they threw out, before the
entry of their hive, ſome ſcores of white young drones ; but,
on the return of fair weather,—inſtead of tearing out and killing the remainder of this unfortunate race, the Queen immediately

times kill them in a more tedious and lingering, but no less effectual way, by banishing them from their granaries of honey; upon which the drones retreat in great numbers to the stool and the under edges of the hive; and sometimes, though rarely, I have even seen them come to the outside of the hive, in small clusters. When thus exiled, they soon become very dull and lifeless, and at last die for want of food. Upon lifting up a hive from the stool, I have observed numbers of them sitting close upon it, with hardly three or four common bees among them, and on such occasions I have trode to death forty, or more of them, at once, with my foot. But, without lifting the hive,

diately laid fresh eggs, in the drone cells, and the common bees again carefully reared them up to maturity.

Whenever, therefore, the young drones are torn out of their cells before swarming time, in bad weather, the bees ought immediately to be fed, which will prevent them from despairing, and save the lives of the young drones.

It is also necessary to mention, that if the weather be bad for two or three days, after a new swarm is introduced into an empty hive, the bees should be fed and encouraged by a little honey; as, in such cases, I have frequently seen them, when long confined, not only soon discouraged, but some of them die; whereas, by being carefully fed, they are not only kept in good spirits, but will, with greater chearfulness, embrace the first favourable moment for resuming their labours.

hive, any perfon may eafily affift the working bees to kill the drones, (as foon as the bees fhow us the example), by fitting down at the fide of the hive the firft good day thereafter, about eleven o'clock, and crufhing them one by one, as they come out of the hive, by preffing them to the ftool with his fore finger. In this manner, an hundred drones may be killed in a very fhort time. I generally kill the moft of the drones in my hives when I have leifure ; although there is no abfolute neceffity for doing it, as the working bees will perform the tafk themfelves in due time. But it certainly occafions a confiderable faving of honey, and I am inclined to think, that no harm can arife from it, efpecially in thofe hives whofe honey is to be taken in Autumn. However, when there are very few drones in a hive I kill none of them ; but when they are very numerous, I often kill fome hundreds ; at leaft two thirds of them, and leave the working bees to kill the reft at their leifure.

C H A P. XXIII.

ADVANTAGES OF CHANGING THE SITUATION OF BEE-HIVES
TO BETTER PASTURE.

ABOUT Lammas, thofe who live in fituations where the vegetation is early over, efpecially if poffeffed of a large number of hives,
ought to remove their bees to the neighbourhood of heath grounds, if they fhould even
be fix or eight miles diftant, and allow them
to continue in that fituation till the heath gives
over bloffoming. This meafure I would earneftly recommend, as the bees, after having
had all the advantage of their early fituations,
will work as late in the feafon, as thofe in the
lateft fituations. I have often feen a hive, by
being placed nigh heath, become ten, twelve,
or fifteen pounds heavier, in the month of Auguft; ‡ whereas, if it had remained in its ori-

A 2

ginal

‡ I can affure my readers, that, in the middle of September
1792, I have feen bees in fuch fituations, filling their hives
with combs and honey, as plentifully and as expeditioufly,

as

ginal early fituation, it would probably have become every day lighter after Lammas. The only rifk in this cafe is, that if the weather turn out bad in Auguft, the bee-mafter will lofe all his trouble; but contingencies of this kind happen in every other bufinefs in which mankind engage, which neverthelefs do not deter us from adventuring.

When bees are placed in a new fituation, they fhould not be permitted to come out of their hives, for the firft time, in cold weather; for, finding themfelves in a ftrange place, they will fly about and take a view of the neighbourhood; and fome of them alighting, and refting on the cold ground, the cold benumbs them, and they perifh, unlefs fpeedily recovered by the heat of the fun. When I remove a hive to a new ftation, I keep them clofe prifoners till the firft fine day, when, about 10 o'-clock A. M.—the time they are moft impatient

to

as if it had been the middle of June. In the beginning of September, that year, I purchafed for a gentleman in Northumberland, a confiderable number of hives, that were only about half full of combs when placed in his apiary; but the heath in his grounds being extremely rich and in full bloffom, the bees were fo expeditious in their labours, that they filled the hives completely with both combs and honey, within a week thereafter.

to get out, I place a feeding comb before their entry, which I at the fame time open, and the bees come out in great numbers, and fly about with great alacrity, making their ufual chearful mufic in the air, for two or three minutes, and taking a view of their new fituation. In the mean time, fome of them difcover the feeding comb, and entertain themfelves with it, while the flying bees alight at the entry, and make their ufual mufic for joy; which invites the ftraggling bees to return home, fo that, perhaps, fcarce a fingle bee of the whole hive will have miffed its way; whereas, if they are allowed to go out fingly, efpecially in cold weather, a confiderable number of bees will be loft, for want of fuch mufic in the air, or at the entry of the hive, to call them home.

In the removal of bees in general, it is better and fafer, to remove a hive to the diftance of a mile or fo, than to a nearer fituation; for, when a hive is removed out of an apiary, where there are a confiderable number of hives, to the diftance of about a quarter of a mile or fo; and efcially, if the bees are allowed to come gradually out of their hives, they will fly to their old place of abode; but not finding their own hive, they will fly about in fearch of it, in a difconfolate

A a 2   manner

manner, for hours perhaps ; and after being repeatedly difappointed, they will at laft try thofe hives that ftand neareft the place where their own hive ftood, to fee if the inhabitants will admit them, as fo many *deftitute orphans*, into their community. When they thus come in a humble fupplicating manner, they are feldom refufed permiffion to enter, and affociate with the reft of the hive, as fellow-labourers. Being favourably received, they are ever after treated, not only as *allies*, but as *brethren* of the fame family, and live in the greateft harmony with them ever after.

Similar meafures ought to be adopted in all cafes of uniting and re-inforcing whatever. If any perfon fhould take a hive out of his own apiary, and drive all the bees out of it, they would fly about in the fame manner, and at laft enter into thofe hives, that would admit them kindly. In fuch cafes, however, the firft ambaffadors, (like thofe of King DAVID to HANUN, the Ammonite,) may, perhaps, be miftaken for SPIES, and treated accordingly. But it will fometimes happen, that the beemafter is in fuch circumftances, that he will be obliged to remove a hive a quarter of a mile from other bees. In this cafe, he muft keep

the

the bees prifoners for fome time, as above-mentioned, efpecially if the hives in the original
appiaries be fhut or covered over, till the bees
of the removed one fly about for an hour or
fo. Thus, the lofs will be the lefs, as perhaps
fome of the ftraggling bees may find their
way back to their own brethren again. But
even although an hundred, or two hundred
bees fhould fly off in this manner, a ftrong
hive will fuffer little by the want of them.

CHAP. XXIV.

OF BEE-BREAD AND WAX.

THE fubftance, commonly called BEE-BREAD,
is to be found at the bottom of many of the
cells, and is frequently covered over with honey. The bees carry it home in loads upon
their legs, or rather their thighs. It is generally of a yellow colour, but often takes its
colour from the flowers from which it is collected.

Various

Various conjectures have been made by different authors respecting its use. Some alledge that the bees eat it; hence the name, *Bee-bread.* Others suppose, that, after being taken into their stomachs, it is converted by some peculiar action of their internal juices into wax, of which every body knows their combs are made. But an objection to this hypothesis, arises from the consideration, that the bees, when first put into an empty hive, carry little or none of this stuff on their legs for some time, till a great number of combs are made; and that after the combs are completed, (which they generally are within two or three weeks after the swarm have taken possession of the hive,) the bees still continue to carry in this stuff during the whole working season. To this, however, it may be replied, that perhaps, as they have no cells to put it into at that time, they carry it home in their bellies, where it probably undergoes a speedy change in passing through their bodies, and may thereby be converted into perfect wax, with which they manufacture their combs.

There is another class of authors, who suppose that the bee-bread is used by the old bees to feed the young ones in the cells, by the

mouth

mouth, as pigeons feed their young ones. To this it may be objected, that the young bees furely cannot make ufe of all the bee-bread, which the old bees are almoft conftantly carrying into the hive when they are at work. Perhaps both thefe laft hypothefes may be true ; as it may not only ferve to feed the young bees, but alfo, by paffing through the bodies of the old ones, may be converted into wax ; with which bees not only build their combs, when a fwarm is newly put into a hive, but alfo feal up both their young in the cells, and their honey in the combs. If this fuppofition be true, then the confumption of bee-bread, through the courfe of the year, but efpecially during the honey and breeding feafons, muft be very great ; and therefore we need not be furprized at the quantities imported by the working bees. But, whatever truth may be in either or both of thefe theories, I am certain of one thing, that the bees do not live on beebread alone ; for they will die of hunger, although there be plenty of it in the hive, if there be no honey in it ; whereas, when they have abundance of honey, they will live without bee-bread, at leaft for many weeks. Reau-

MUR

MUR, however, fays, that it is abfolutely neceffary for food to bees.

For my part, I have always obferved the bees
moft bufily employed in carrying in this ftuff
while the young bees are breeding ; but when
they want a Queen, and have no eggs to rear
another, they immediately give over carrying
it into the hive, thinking, (as it would feem,)
that as they have no young bees to feed or feal
up in the cells, it would be an idle bufinefs to
bring any more of it home, efpecially as they
do not make much ufe of it themfelves, and
have more already in the hive than they will
ftand in need of, for their own ufe. Mr
Thorley alledges, that the bees carry the wax
home from the fields in fine fmall fcales‡ between the folds of their bodies. He fays, that
" For feveral feafons, after I became a Bee-ma-
" fter, I was very defirous and diligent to find
" out how, or where, they brought home their
" wax, well knowing that grofs matter to be of
" a very contrary nature, and applied to fome
                                        " other

‡ Thefe fcales are well known by bee-mafters, and fomewhat
refemble fmall falt at a diftance, but, upon a nearer infpection,
they are more like the fcales of very fmall fifh, being thin, fmall,
round and white. Their fubftance is nothing but pure wax.

" other ufe, but was not able for a confiderable
" time, to enter into the fecret.

" At laft, viewing a hive of bees very bufy
" at labour, I obferved one bee among the reft,
" as fhe fixed upon the alighting place, of an
" unufual appearance ; upon which I feized
" her directly, before fhe had time to enter the
" hive ; where, with a very fenfible pleafure, I
" found what I had (till then) been in vain
" fearching for. Upon the belly of this bee,
" within the plaits, were fixed no lefs than fix
" pieces of folid wax, perfectly white and tran-
" fparent like gum ; three upon one fide, and
" three upon the other, appearing to the eye e-
" qual in bulk and gravity ; fo that the body
" of the bee feemed duly poifed, and the flight
" not in the leaft obftructed by any inequali-
" ties.

" Here have I found it at other times, and
" once I took away eight pieces together, and I
" knew that it was wax, and nothing elfe. Will
" not this pafs for demonftration ?"

That Mr THORLEY, and probably fome o-
thers, have feen bees carrying fuch white fcales,
or pieces of folid wax, on their bodies, once
or twice perhaps in their lives, I will not dif-

B b   pute.

pute. I myfelf have feen the fame phænomenon,
once, or at moft twice, during an experience of
thirty years.   But it certainly would be abfurd
to infer from thefe rare cafes, that all the wax,
which the combs are made of, is carried into
the hive in this manner.   The contrary inference muft be drawn, were it from nothing elfe
but the confideration, that thefe white fcales
have been fo very feldom obferved.   It is alfo
well known, that when a young fwarm is newly fet down, within a fhort time thereafter,
fmall fcales of fine white wax will be feen on
the ftool; which is a certain proof that the bees
are beginning to build combs : and perhaps a
few of the bees may pick up fome of thefe fcales,
to prevent them from being loft.   But, if every
bee, that is employed in carrying wax for building the combs, either within or on the outfide
of her body, could be obferved, we would fee
thoufands thus loaded every day after a young
fwarm is firft fet down, inftead of obferving
only one or two folitary inftances in the courfe
of twenty or thirty years.

If a natural or artificial fwarm is confined
24 hours in a hive, after it is newly put into
it, the bees will be found bufily employed in
making combs.   From this it may be argued,
that

that the bees, having eaten a quantity of bee
bread on purpofe, before they left their own
hive, and having it ftill in their ftomachs, had
made wax of it to erect the combs.

Of this fact any perfon may convince himfelf, by driving the bees out of any hive into
an empty one, and confining them 24 hours ;
after which, upon examining the hive attentively, he will find a piece of comb, perhaps fix or
eight inches long, befides feveral hundreds of
fcales lying on the ftool. It is evident, then,
that thefe fcales could not be brought from the
field, as Mr THORLEY fuppofes, feeing the
bees were never out of the hive ; and, it is farther to be obferved, that when they are at full
liberty to work in the fields, and when a young
fwarm is moft bufily employed in rearing
combs, nothing can be feen on their bodies of
thefe fcales, or any thing elfe.

I have fometimes, indeed, been inclined to
think, that the wax might be an excrefcence,
exudation, or production from the bodies of
the bees ; and that, as the Queen bee can lay
eggs when fhe pleafes, if need require, fo the
working bees can produce wax from the fubftance of their own bodies. If this conjecture
be right, it will follow of courfe, that all the

food

food which the bees take, contributes to the for-
mation of wax, in the fame manner as all the
food which a cow eats contributes to the production of milk: or, (to adopt a more near fi-
mile from the infect tribe,) as all the food
which a fpider takes, contributes not only to
the nourifhment of the animal, but to the production of the fubftance of the cob-web from its
body. Numberlefs other analogies in nature
might be adduced in favour of the probability
of this theory. The filk, for inftance, produced
from the body of the filk worm, is a fubftance as
different from that of the animal itfelf, or of the
mulberry leaf it feeds on, as wax is from that
of the body of the bee, or of the honey or flower fhe fucks. And the excrefcence produced
in the human ear, which alfo goes by the name
of *wax*, is certainly a fubftance as different
from that of the body which produces it, as
either the one or the other. Upon the whole,
until I meet with a more probable theory, fup-
ported by facts, I muft give it as my humble
opinion, that the wax is either produced from
the bodies of the bees alone, or rather that the
bees can fpeedily convert what they bring from
the flowers into it, and therewith build their
combs, and feal up both their young and their
honey.   CHAP.

CHAP. XXV.

OF THE HONEY HARVEST.

I ONCE thought, that if we preferve all our bees, we muft alfo keep all our honey in the hives, to maintain them during winter and fpring. But I am now of a different opinion; for the feverity of the winter not only reduces the number of bees, but fometimes even kills whole hives, although they have large quantities of honey in them. It is, therefore, much more profitable to preferve all the bees alive, and unite them to other hives, although we fhould be at the expence of fome honey to feed them during fpring. It is indeed, probable, that every Queen is capable of laying only a certain number of eggs. Suppofing, then, that we fhould put 100,000 common bees in a hive, the old bees would gradually die out, and as there would be but one breeding Queen in the hive, it would foon have no more bees than

any

any other hive. Indeed, experience convinces me, that there never was a hive, however large, profperous, and numerous of inhabitants in fummer, either naturally, or by being united, that did not gradually decreafe againft next fpring, fo as very little to exceed the moft ordinary hives in number. It is true, indeed, that fome fwarms of bees, by being kept in a very large hive for feveral years, have had as much honey and wax, as three or four ordinary hives. But fuch cafes only occur, either when two or three fwarms go together in fwarming time, or when a thriving fwarm continues for fome years in a large hive; and, by collecting perhaps 6olb. of honey every year, and confuming only the half of it during winter and fpring, thus increafes the ftock of honey, and the weight of the hives, at the rate of 3olb. a-year*.

Neverthelefs

---

* I am quite certain, however, that a great number of bees in one capacious hive,—I fhall fuppofe 30,000,—will breed amazingly; as they will have perhaps, in June or July, not under 7,000 young in the cells; for almoft every comb in the hive at that feafon, will be quite full of eggs, nymphs and young bees, all gradually coming forward. According to this calculation, allowing 18 days to pafs between the time that an egg is laid, and a complete bee produced from it, there would not be fewer than 300 eggs laid each day in the hive,—an aftonifhing numbe

Neverthelefs it is evident, that a hive that has a great number of bees in autumn, ftands

a

her to be all laid by one mother. Monfieur REAUMUR fays, that the Queen will lay 200 in 24 hours ; but I am perfuaded, that, in fome extraordinarily populous hives, fhe lays near double that number. She is acknowledged by all authors to be very prolific. SWAMMERDANE beheld in the ovarium of a Queen bee, 5100 eggs at once ; and REAUMUR fays, that, " in the fpace of " three weeks, 6000 bees are brought to perfection." Nor, indeed, is this at all incredible, when we confider that fome cod fifh have had no fewer than 9,344,000 eggs in their ovarium at once. * The prolific powers of the Queen bee feem to depend very much on the ftate of the hive fhe belongs to ; and I am apt to think, that the increafe of a hive fcarcely ever fails on her part, if fhe be in a healthy ftate. For, during the months of May, June, and July, all Queens breed furprifingly faft, if the weather is good, and if they have abundance of common bees to rear the young brood. When one, therefore, has a hive, that, on account of the paucity of its inhabitants, does not breed faft, were he to add a great number of common bees to it in Summer, it would foon increafe as faft as any in his apiary.

It muft, however, be allowed, that fome Queens will be more fruitful than others, although a hive feldom fuffers from that caufe alone. One fingle author alledges, that two or three Queens may be permitted to live for a fhort time in a hive, during the middle of fummer, and that of courfe a greater number of eggs will be laid each day, than if there were but one Queen in the hive. But I am pretty confident, that this is a miftake ; for, among the many hundreds of fwarms, which I have driven out, I never faw more than one breeding Queen at a time. Indeed, perhaps, in one hive among fifty, I have obferved two

Queens,

* Nature delineated, p. 130.

a much better chance not to perish by the feverity of the winter, than a hive that has not half the number of inhabitants; for which reafon I would earneftly recommend it to my readers, NEVER TO KILL A SINGLE WORKING BEE, at any feafon of the year; but, in autumn, to unite all the bees of thofe hives, from which the honey is taken, to thofe that are intended to be kept as ftock hives. This will render them fit to defend themfelves both againft the feverity of the weather in winter, and againft robbers in fpring; and will alfo greatly forward their labours as foon as the working feafon returns; for, as has been already obferved, it is of the greateft importance to have the hives always well-ftored with bees.

The time of taking the honey out of the hives is fometimes earlier, and fometimes later, according to the weather, and the earlinefs or latenefs of the flowers in the neighbourhood.

I

Queens, an old and a young one; but that hive would have fent off the young Queen with a new fwarm probably in a day or two, as fhe was only waiting an opportunity for that purpofe; and it may be obferved, that the young Queen was not then arrived at the age of laying eggs, as fhe is about eight days old before fhe can become a mother; and therefore I am fully perfuaded, that there are never on any occafion two Queens in the fame hive, laying eggs at one time.

I have known a hive of bees waſte their honey, and the hive become gradually lighter after the firſt week of Auguſt; and, at other times, in favourable weather, I have ſeen hives of bees, that were ſituated near heath, (as mentioned, page 185) continue working keenly during the whole of Auguſt, and the greater part of September, and become daily heavier. In a word, the harveſt of honey, like that of corn, is earlier or later, more plentiful or ſcarce, in different years, according to the weather and the climate, and the variety of ſeaſons and ſituations.

One general rule, however, may be laid down for the proper time to take honey. As ſoon as the flowers, in the neighbourhood of an apiary, are moſtly faded, although the bees may continue to work in favourable days, yet their families being now generally very large, they will probably conſume as much honey in one day, as they will collect in two. At this period, therefore, the prudent bee-maſter will firſt chooſe his ſtock hives, according to the directions given, page 89. He will then put a mark on every hive he has picked out for this purpoſe, and ſell or take the honey from all the reſt, whether good or bad; for the ſooner the honey is taken, it will run the more eaſily out

C c of

of the combs. And, as it runs beſt in warm weather, he ſhould take the honey, that he intends to run out of the combs, immediately after the bees have nearly given over work, and unite the bees to his ſtock hives, as directed page 136, &c.

But honey, that is intended to be kept in the combs, ought not to be taken ſo ſoon, as cold weather renders the combs more fit to be handled; and as the bees are all to be kept alive, and of courſe muſt be maintained, it is of no conſequence, in point of expence, whether they are allowed to feed on the honey in the hive they are ſoon to leave, or on that of the hive to which they are to be united. Beſides, there is an additional advantage, that ariſes from their being allowed to continue in their native hive; as the longer they remain in it, the more young bees will be hatched; which both preſerves a greater number of bees, and makes the honey combs more free of the young brood; ſo that there is no harm in keeping the bees in the hives till October, when the honey is not intended to be run out of them.

When the honey of a hive is taken in Autumn, and there is a great number of young in the cells, thoſe combs which contain the young,

and

and which may be intermingled with bee-bread,
ſhould be carefully and gently placed in an eek,
(ſee page 110, &c.), and a numerous hive put
over it, to hatch out the young brood, and ſuck
up the particles of honey remaining in the
combs, and probably alſo make ſome uſe of
the bee-bread. This plan is of great advantage
to the bee-maſter, as the young bees, which are
always the beſt, and which would otherwiſe
have been totally loſt, will thus be all pre-
ſerved; beſides that very little uſe could have
been made of ſuch honey in the cells, as was
mixed with young bees, eggs, and bee-bread.
The eek and the combs may be removed in a-
bout three or four weeks thereafter, and the
hive ſet down in its former ſtation.

If the bee-maſter has not as many good
hives as he wiſhes to keep for ſtock, he may ſupply himſelf, by conjoining the bees and honey of
two light hives, and uniting them into one in
September, as mentioned in page 47. The hea-
vieſt hive ſhould be firſt ſelected; after which,
the bees and honey ſhould be taken out of the
light hives in the following manner:

The Bee-maſter muſt firſt drive as many of
the bees as poſſible into an empty hive, as di-

rected in page 138. But, at this period, and
in all cold ſeaſons, bees are not ſo eaſily driven
out as in warm weather; although, the taking
them into a warm room, will make them run
up the better. Afterwards, he ſhould take the
combs carefully out, eſpecially if it be a light
young hive, one by one, with his hand; and,
in doing this, all the bees that are upon the
combs may be gently ſwept off with a large
feather, into the hive, among their brethren.
Their Queen muſt then be taken away, with a-
bout 100 bees, and kept cloſe priſoners; then
re-inforce any hive with the common bees that
appears to have feweſt inhabitants in it, (as directed p. 136, &c.) or rather any hive that will
give them the moſt favourable reception; and,
as ſoon as all the bees are united and happy,
the Queen, with her hundred attendants, may
be introduced; and, if they judge her to be
preferable to their own, (for the bees are doubt-
leſs the beſt judges in theſe matters) perhaps
they will elect her and baniſh their own
Queen. About two days thereafter, the hive
intended for the ſtock may be re-inforced with
the honey combs; according to the directions
given in pages 110, 111, and 112.

The Bee-maſter ſhould proceed in the ſame
manner

manner with every other hive, from which he intends to take honey ; and if any of his neigh- bours ſhould happen to be ſtill ſo prejudiced in favour of old cuſtoms, as to continue the bar- barous practice of killing their bees, he may make an advantageous bargain with them, and ſave the lives of the useful inſects, by offering a trifle for them, which will ſurely be accepted, as the owners can otherwiſe gain nothing by them. By uniting theſe to his own hives, eve- ry hive in his apiary will be fully ſupplied with bees and honey: And being now in a proſpe- rous ſtate, may be carefully covered over, and rendered fit to endure the winter. See page 97.

CHAP. XXVI.

OF PREPARING HONEY AND WAX.

Before entering upon this neceſſary buſineſs, the bee-maſter ſhould be properly provided with a ſufficient number of utenſils, ſuch as large diſhes, jars, ſieves, knives and ſpoons. He ſhould begin while the honey is warm, as

it

it will run from the combs the more quickly;
and therefore, to preferve the heat till the operation is over, the hive fhould be brought into
a warm room. He fhould next take hold of
the ends of the crofs fticks in the hive with
pincers, and loofen them by twifting them
round; after which they will be eafily pulled
out. The edges of the combs fhould then be
loofened with a knife from the hive all around.
Upon giving the hive a gentle knock on the
floor, on that fide which is oppofite to the
broad fide of the combs, they will fall to that
fide, and upon turning the hive, and giving it
another knock on the oppofite fide, all the
combs, which could be reached by the knife
will be effectually loofened. The hive being
ftill kept on its broad fide, the combs will all
be above each other. The uppermoft being
firft taken off, if there are any dead bees in it,
they may be blown or brufhed off. The combs
fhould then be divided into three parts. The
empty combs being firft laid afide for wax;
next the combs containing eggs or maggots;
and laftly, the moft valuable part of the whole,
the fine fealed combs, containing the honey,
fhould be laid in a veffel by themfelves. An
affiftant fhould immediately be ordered to cut
                                              thefe

thefe laft into thin flices, firft obferving to pare off the fealed mouths of the cells, that the honey may run freely out. In this ftate they fhould be laid in fieves, or any other veffels that will afford a free paffage to the honey, which will run quite clear, and the honey thus obtained fhould be kept by itfelf, as being the pureft and beft.

Thofe combs which may be filled with a mixture of live young maggots, bee-bread and honey, fhould immediately * be put below ftock hives, as directed page 202, &c. and the bees will foon fuck up all the honey in them. When the fine combs are completely run, they fhould be put into a pan, over a flow fire, and ftirred conftantly till they are more than milk warm; when they fhould be put into a ftrong canvafs bag, and the honey fqueezed out. This honey being of an inferior quality, may be either ufed in the family, for common ufes; or rather kept for feeding the bees. All the combs, from which it was fqueezed, may then be foaked in water, and a weak kind of mead

---

* All combs containing eggs and young in the cells muft be put immediately to other hives, while they are warm; for, fhould they remain two or three hours out of a hive, they will become chill and cool, fo as to make them decay in the cells.

mead drawn from them; or a ftronger mead may be taken from the combs by foaking them, after the fineft of the honey is run off, without melting or fqueezing them at all. Indeed, in warm weather, fine combs will run almoft quite dry, without the leaft preffure.

My method of running honey is this : I hang up a wide riddle, with the fliced honey combs in it, about 5 feet from the ground : About 8 or 10 inches below this, I place a fieve, fomewhat wider in circumference than the riddle, and, at an equal diftance under the fieve, a fine fearch, proportionally wider than the fieve, under which, a foot lower ftill, I place one of my earthen covers, defcribed page 98, with the bottom uppermoft, and a fmall hole in the top, to anfwer the purpofe of a funnel. This laft being properly fixed in a veffel of a fufficient fize, the honey that runs into it is completely purified from all extraneous matter whatever, by running through fo many different fieves at one time. Thus, in a few hours, in a warm day, I can have my honey purified to the higheft degree of finenefs, without boiling or diluting it, or ufing any other means that would deprive it of its original genuine flavour ; for any fmall crumbs of wax, bee-bread or the like, that pafs through the

the riddle, are caught by the fieve ; and if any thing ftill fmaller fhould pafs through the fieve, it is intercepted by the fearch, which permits nothing but the pureft honey to pafs through the funnel into the receiving veffel; and thus the whole procefs is completed in a fhort time. During this procefs, the combs in the riddle may now and then be turned over with a knife, to make the honey run the more freely.

This method fhould be adopted by all Bee-mafters, who have many hives and much honey to run. But fuch as have but a fmall quantity may follow the other plan, and their honey will do very well, if they only keep it free of young bees and bee-bread : for a few crumbs of wax running through the fieve will not hurt the honey, as it will foon rife to the furface, and can be eafily fkimmed off.

The combs being now entirely free of honey, the next operation neceffary is to make wax. My method of performing this is quite fimple. I boil the combs in a kettle, with a fufficient quantity of water, over a flow fire, for about 40 minutes, during which time they are all melted, and I ftir them about frequently all the time. I then take two or three ladle-fulls, and put into a bag, fewed together in

D d the

the form of a funnel, and which is commonly called *Hippocrates's Lever*. It is made of thin ſtrong canvaſs, and of ſuch a length, that the upper part may come over the end of a board, which leans upon my breaſt, while the other end of it is placed in a veſſel fit to receive the wax, from which I preſs out the water and the wax, pretty much in the ſame way that the tanners dreſs their leather.

I generally boil what remains in the bag a ſecond time, and ſqueeze it again to obtain more wax. By this method, however, the wax cannot be got entirely out of the droſs ; nor indeed can it be obtained by any other mode that I have ever ſeen or heard of being attempted. All the wax that is ultimately left among the droſs, in this way of ſeparating it, is of very little value, and would not refund the expence of any further trouble. *

After the wax is cooled in the tub, I again put it into the kettle with clean water, and having

* I have tried ſeveral other methods, in order to extract all the wax from the droſs. Near twenty years ago, I got a preſs made for this purpoſe, ſomewhat reſembling thoſe which the candle-makers uſe to ſqueeze their tallow with ; but, finding it did not anſwer the purpoſe, I laid it aſide. I have alſo put in practice Mr Keys's method, but, after repeated trials, found it not ſatisfactory.

ing melted it, I pour it into a bowl or veffel, ‡ which is wider at the top than at the
bottom, and fkim off any drofs that may float
on the top of the wax. After allowing it to
ftand in fome warm place, that it may cool gradually, which prevents it from cracking, I take
out the cake of wax, and pare off all the drofs
from the under fide, till there be nothing
left but what is fit for the merchant. The
fkimmings and parings fhould be kept and
boiled over again, next time any more wax is
made, in order to obtain as much wax as poffible.

‡ **A** veffel made fomething like a flower pot, that is both narrow and deep, anfwers beft for this purpofe : as the good wax
rifes to the top, and the droffy part is much more eafily feparated
from it, than when the veffel is broad and fhallow ; as in this
cafe, the cake of wax is thin, and not fo eafily feparated from the
drofs, when cold.

CHAP.

CHAP. XXVII.

OF THE DIFFERENT KINDS OF HONEY.

IT appears that honey does not candy from cold alone, without fome other concurring circumftances; for among a number of hives, all equally expofed to the fame degree of cold, fome will be found to have candied honey in them, while others have none. Even in the fame hive, a comb will fometimes be found, with honey in it, partly candied and partly liquid: And it is well known, that fome honey will turn thick and candy, almoft as foon as it is run out of the cells, fo early as the month of Auguft; while other honey will continue liquid till November, December, or January: And fome very fine honey will remain till April, before it candy. From all thefe facts, it muft be inferred, that there are other concurring circumftances befides cold, that co-operate with it in occafioning honey to candy. What thefe circumftances are, it is difficult to determine.

mine. My opinion is, that the candying of honey proceeds partly from the nature of the flowers from which it is collected, and partly from the time that it has remained in the hive. But againſt this laſt ſuppoſition an objection ariſes, from this conſideration, that the very fineſt of what is called *virgin honey*, will ſometimes candy very ſoon after it has run from the combs, and become like fine white ſugar *.

This fine white honey is collected from white clover, and alſo from ſome other flowers which yield a white juice, and it is reckoned by moſt people the fineſt of honey. But the ſpecies of honey which continues longeſt in a liquid ſtate, and

---

* Many authors affirm, that honey, candied in the comb, is very deſtructive to bees, and alledge, that they may as well eat poiſon; others inſiſt, that it chokes them; while a third claſs alledge, that it hurts them by bedaubing them, with many other whimſical ſuppoſitions. But theſe authors certainly have either taken their own dreams for realities, or have wrote upon truſt; which they certainly ought not, in a caſe that can be ſo eaſily decided by experiment. For let any perſon put a piece of comb into a hive, with the honey in the cells, partly candied and partly liquid, and he will find, that the bees will ſoon ſuck up all the liquid honey in the upper parts of the cells; and if the middle part of the honey be candied, they will throw it out, and thus get at the liquid honey in the under parts;—which they will chearfully feed upon, without either choking, bedaubing, or poiſoning themſelves with it, and rejoice that they have got ſo much proviſion at ſo little expence of time and labour.

and is efteemed by many connoiffeurs the very beft of honey, (as it undoubtedly is as good
as any,) is of a flightly greenifh colour, and is
likewife collected from white flowers. When
candied, it fometimes confifts of fine white particles, refembling fmall hail, intermixed with
fome liquid honey, and is very beautiful.

Heath produces a fine high-coloured honey,
which looks alfo very beautiful in the virgin
comb, fhining like gold through the pure tranfparent cells. The gentlemen and ladies about
Newcaftle are very fond of this kind of honey in
the combs. When run into pots and candied,
it becomes all hard and griftly,—a fpecies
of honey which is alfo greatly efteemed by
many.

There is another kind of honey, which is collected from all the above-mentioned flowers,
and which, having been kept two or three years
in the hive, is therefore called *old honey.* Some
of that kind of honey will be very fine tafted,
and pretty griftly when eat, but the greateft
part of it, when it is run out of the combs,
becomes in a few days thereafter thick and
fmooth ; and is, on that account, fufpected, by
people who are ignorant of the nature of honey, to have been adulterated, and mixed up
                                                    with

with butter, fugar, flower, and the like. This
miftake prevails in many parts of the country,
and it is much to be regretted ; as this fufpi-
cion, fo injurious to the characters of honeft
country people, who, in reality, fell their honey
as it run from the combs, is even fometimes
entertained by perfons in the higher ranks of
life, who might be expected to be better informed. For although the country dealers fometimes fpoil their honey, by fqueezing out the
combs, and thereby occafioning bee-bread,
eggs, &c. to mingle with it ; yet in all my experience, I have never met with any honey,
which I could difcover to have been mixed with
butter, fugar or flour. Once indeed, and only
once, I faw honey which the owner had mixed
with water, but he was juftly punifhed for his
avarice ; for the honey and water, fomented by
the carriage in fuch a manner, that the upper
part of it had more the appearance of barm or
yeft than of honey ; and the unfortunate dealer loft both his cargo and his character.

Some alledge, that honey may be purified by
warming or boiling it in pots, &c. which occafions it to throw up a fcum, that is fkimmed
off. But I am perfuaded, that honey is always
beft in its natural ftate ; and that fuch methods

of

of refining it, inftead of improving the honey, often communicate a bad tafte or flavour to it. I therefore ufe no other method with my honey, than to let it run freely from the combs, as above, and take particular care, that none of the eggs or bee-bread, get amongft it. And indeed this is all the art which is required to make the very fineft of honey ;—namely, cleanlinefs : Let it only be keep as clean as the bees kept it, and the fineft of honey will be the produce.

CHAP. XXVIII.

OF THE VARIOUS ENEMIES OF BEES, AND HOW TO GUARD AGAINST THEM.

Of all the enemies the bees have hitherto had to encounter, MAN may juftly be confidered as the greateft. For while he follows the old barbarous cuftom of killing whole hives of that induftrious race, for the fake of their honey, (a cuftom which, in many nations, has begun to yield to a more œconomical, as well as a more

humane

humane practice,) he certainly deftroys more of thefe his faithful fervants, annually, than a- ny other clafs of animals whatever, or, indeed, than all the other beafts, birds, and infects u- nited, ever did. Nor are thofe prejudiced mur- derers of the bees, their only enemies among mankind. The predatory clafs, who fteal ei- ther their honey, or the whole hives, prove e- qually deftructive to them. But it is to be hop- ed, that as felf intereft and humanity equally unite in exploding the practice of the murder- ers, fo the effectual execution of the laws will prove a fufficient protection from the thieves†.

The three next greateft enemies of the bees are, Cold, Famine, and Robbers of their own fpecies: To which may be added, as the fourth moft deftructive clafs of enemies, mice. By one or other of thefe, or all of them united, hundreds of hives of bees perifh annually in Britain, while their other enemies hurt them but rarely or partially.

E e   Of

---

† Perhaps I can boaft of a degree of good fortune, in this re- fpect, that fcarcely one in the kingdom can equal; for, notwith- ftanding the great number of bee-hives I have had ftanding in the midft of muirs, and far from any houfes, I never had a fingle hive ftolen but one, nor ever loft one fingle fwarm to my knowledge, by their flying away in fwarming time:

Of the former, we need fay nothing here, having already given fufficient directions in the preceding part of this work, how to guard againft cold, famine, robbers, and mice ; and fhall, therefore, proceed to point out fome of the latter.

Wasps are great enemies to bees, efpecially in warm dry years ; and thofe hives that are near plantations, where they often refort, are the greateft fufferers by them. In my neighbourhood, wafps are feldom very troublefome, except that fometimes a mother wafp will appear before a hive in May, and offer to go in ; but her hoarfe voice and ftrange drefs foon difcover her to the bees, who banifh her from their habitation. I know not if any hive in my neighbourhood was ever much hurt by wafps ; but, a few miles diftant from this, fundry hives have been fometimes confiderably the worfe of them.

The beft way to extirpate wafps is to deftroy their Queen or mother, in fpring, wherever fhe can be found ; for wafps, in this refpect, as well as in fome other particulars, refemble bees ; and therefore, when a mother wafp is killed, a whole neft of them is in effect deftroyed. Their nefts, however, fhould alfo be carefully fought out, and

and as many of them deftroyed as poffible, by burning, fcalding, or drowning them; left, like the bees, the wafps fhould alfo poffefs the power of raifing a Queen mother from a common egg.

When a number of wafps attempt to enter any, hive about the end of fummer or beginning of autumn, the entry fhould be reduced to half an inch in length, and fcarce as much in height, that the bees may be able to defend it; and thofe hives that have but few bees in them fhould be taken, and their bees united to other hives, as directed page 141, &c. But fuch as are intended for ftock hives, if feverely attacked by wafps, fhould be removed to fome fituation diftant from plantations, and kept there, till the feafon of plundering, by both wafps and bees, is over. Veffels may alfo be placed in the apiary, with honey or fugar in them mixed with ale, which will allure and deftroy the wafps; but in fine days thefe veffels fhould be removed, left they fhould likewife allure and deftroy the bees. Another difadvantage alfo frequently attends this method of deftroying the wafps; as thefe veffels, placed in apiaries, are apt to attract all the wafps in the neighbourhood, and thus, by bringing hundreds that would not otherwife have come,

render

render the remedy worfe than the difeafe. This
fhould, therefore, be cautioufly avoided; and
indeed, in general, this method is of no great
fervice.

The large moth, called the WAX MOTH, from
its maggots feeding on the wax, is another
great enemy of the bees. This animal is extremely alert at difcovering any crevice, about
the outfide of the fkirts of the hive, to depofit
her eggs in; and when unfuccefsful in fuch
attempts, fhe nimbly runs in at the entry, un-
perceived by the bees, and lays her eggs, which
quickly become large white maggots, above
half an inch each in length. Thefe maggots
fpin over themfelves a covering for their defence, and become very numerous in fome
hives. Their depredations difcourage the bees
fo much, that they fometimes defert the hive.

For my own part, I never fuffered the fmalleft lofs by thefe invaders: I never faw one of
their maggots in any of my hives, except twice
or thrice, that I obferved a few of them in one
hive; and I never heard any bee-mafter in my
neighbourhood complain of them. But, a-
bout twenty miles diftant, I once faw a dozen
of wax moths in one hive; and the owner told
me, that he had once two hives in one feafon,
which

which had as many of theſe moth maggots in
them as bees ; for which reaſon he burnt them
both, with their bees, combs, honey, wax
moths and maggots altogether. In doing this
he thought he acted prudently ; but, in my o-
pinion, he would have acted a much wiſer
part, if he had driven all the bees that were in
them, into empty hives and made two ſwarms
of them, or re-inforced weak hives, with them ;
and then ſmoaked the wax moths and maggots to death : after which, he might have
given the bees of his other hives the combs to
ſuck the honey from them, and then melted
the wax. His empty hive could have ſerved
another year, and thus he would have ſuffered
no loſs whatever, except that of the young bees,
which would have been very trifling in com-
pariſon of loſing all. The pooreſt and weakeſt
hives are moſt infeſted with wax moths, as well
as with other enemies. When any ſigns of ſuch
vermin appear, either without or within a hive,
they ſhould be inſtantly deſtroyed.

BIRDS of different kinds are alſo enemies to
bees ; eſpecially in Spring, when they catch
them on purpoſe to feed their young with; ſuch
as the ſwallow, the ſparrow, the lark, the duck,
and even the common hen. I myſelf have
ſeen

feen hens pick up bees ; but they very feldom hurt them much. Birds, in general, however, ought to be guarded againft by all poffible means. A fcare-crow placed near a hive will fometimes frighten away the wild birds.

SPIDERS likewife deftroy fome bees by catching them in their nets and fucking their blood ; though a ftrong bee will fometimes break through the flimfy texture, and efcape. Nothing is eafier than to protect them from this enemy, by deftroying the cob-webs as foon as they appear about the hives, or their ftools or covers.

EARWIGS are alfo formidable enemies to bees ; and Mr Keys fays, that " they fteal into " the hive at night and drag out bee after bee, " fucking out their vitals, and leaving nothing " but their fkins, like fo many fcalps or trophies " of their butchery." They breed between the fkirts of the hive and the ftool, where their nefts ought to be fearched for and deftroyed.

" ANTS, (fays Mr WILDMAN,) fometimes " make their nefts between the hive and the " covering, without molefting the bees or be- " ing molefted." Although, for my own part, I was never fenfible of my bees receiving any

injury

injury from ants, yet I have heard some bee-masters say, that they go into hives during the night, and suck the honey; and that they have seen hives ruined by them. To guard against such possible depredations, the covers should be now and then removed, in the end of Summer, and the ants destroyed.

WOOD-LICE are also hurtful to bees. When old decayed wood, which they harbour in, happens to be near a hive, either the wood should be removed to a distance, or the wood-lice carefully searched for and extirpated.

BAD WEATHER, wind, rain, and the extremes of cold and heat, &c. have already been repeatedly noticed as prejudicial to bees, and may be guarded against by the situations of the apiaries, covering the hives properly, &c.

NOISE is also somewhat hurtful to bees, as it disturbs them in their industrious operations. This can likewise be in general easily prevented, by placing the hives in a quiet situation, remote from noisy operations, high ways and the like.

To conclude,—FILTH and IMPURITY of every kind that may gather upon the stool, or around the outside of the hive, or be introduced near the hive, so as to occasion disagreeable effluvia,

effluvia, ought to be carefully removed and guarded againft, by keeping the hives and every thing near them perfectly fweet and clean.

CHAP. XXIX.

CONCLUSION.

As the principal intention of this work is to ftimulate the attention of the public towards an important object, that has been hitherto too much neglected, I fhall conclude with a few words of advice to people of all ranks and degrees amongft us, on the fubject.

And, *firft*, I would humbly advife all GEN-TLEMEN of LANDED PROPERTY, to confider, whether they have not multitudes of mellifluous flowers growing in many places of their grounds, which might yield annually feveral hundred pints of honey, as well as many pounds of wax, with very little trouble or expence, but whofe fweets being overlooked and neglected, ferve only to feed the caterpillars and the wafps.

In

In the next place, I would feriously advife every CLERGYMAN, whether belonging to the eftablifhed church, or to any other fect or party, to keep a few bee hives in his garden, or upon his giebe. I have for feveral years paft paid a clergyman's lady in my neighbourhood fome pounds for honey and wax, which fhe had to fpare after her own family was ferved. I have, in my poffeffion, two books on the fubject of bees, wrote by two clergymen, one of whom had EIGHTY SIX fwarms in one year.

Mr Wheeler likewife informs us, that while he was viewing the beauties of Parnaffus, he was entertained by a clergyman with the fweets of a repaft of honey. " After I had difcourfed " fome time," fays he †, " with the good old " Caloyer, (Prieft) whom they efteemed a Saint, I " was conducted into a garden well planted with " beans and peas, (this was at the end of Janu- " ary,) and another by it, furnifhed with four " or five hundred ftocks of bees. The good old " Caloyer prefently went, took a ftock of bees, " and brought me a little of delicate white ho- " ney combs, with bread and olives, and very

F f " good

† A Journey into Greece, by George Wheeler, Efq; in company with Dr Spon of Lyons, p. 411.

" good wine; to which he set us down in his
" hut, and made us a dinner, with far greater
" satisfaction than the most princely banquet
" in Europe could have afforded us."

That the number of our hives might be
greatly increased, wherever there is proper pasture for bees, appears evidently from Mr Wheeler's narrative, and is confirmed by the following passage in the account lately published of
the sheep in Spain.

" If sheep loved aromatic plants, it would be
" one of the greatest misfortunes that could be-
" fal the farmers in Spain. The number of
" bee-hives there is incredible. I am almost
" ashamed to give under my hand, that I knew
" a parish priest who had five thousand hives."

GENTLEMEN FARMERS ought, therefore, by
no means to neglect the culture of bees. They
have almost as many advantages as the proprietors themselves. The great quantities of clover,
mustard, and heath, with which their grounds
in general abound, would maintain a bee-hive
for every horse and cow they have upon their
grounds. And gentlemen STORE-MASTERS
might keep at least a couple of hives for every
score of sheep they have in their sheep-walks.
Indeed, farmers of every rank will find their
advantage

advantage in keeping bee-hives, in proportion
to the extent of the flowers that grow upon their
farms; as one single acre, planted with turnips,
muſtard, clover, or heath, will feed many hives.
Even the meaneſt cottager, who has but a cot-
tage and a kail-yard, might keep two or three
hives, and ſow a little muſtard and turnips, or
plant a few gooſeberry buſhes, on purpoſe to feed
his bees. There is ſcarce a country village in the
kingdom, that might not afford to keep as many
bee-hives as there are dwelling houſes in it; nor
a tradeſman in ſuch a village, who might not eaſily keep as many hives as he has hands employed in his buſineſs. Even ſervants might have
a few hives kept as their own property, in the
gardens of their parents, brothers, or friends.
In ſhort, perſons of all ranks and degrees, from
the KING to the cottager, might be profitably
employed, or agreeably amuſed, by keeping bee-
hives †.

F f 2

Let

† I am quite certain, and ſome others have often told me,
that they were of the ſame opinion, that the melodious humming
of bees, when buſy at work, or ſporting in the air for their
own amuſement, will have ſuch an effect upon the animal ſpirits,
that, however chagrined or ruffled the temper of a perſon might
be, before he takes a walk among his bees, he generally does
not withdraw till the mind enjoys a perfect calm and inward tran-
quillity.

Let none here alledge, that thefe our induſtrious infects are below the attention of the
greateſt. MELISSUS, the firſt inventor of bee-
hives, was a king; but perhaps we ſhould never
have heard of him, if he had not paid particular attention to thefe his little ſubjects. Encouragement might alſo be given to the culture of
bees, by reſpectable ſocieties, ſuch as the Board
of Agriculture, the Highland Society, &c. who
might advertiſe ſmall premiums, to be given
to thoſe who ſhould rear the greateſt number of hives, or bring the greateſt quantity of
honey and wax to the market during the ſeaſon. Perſons properly qualified might alſo be
employed, either by ſocieties or individuals, to
inſpect the ſtate of the hives within certain diſ-
tricts. One perſon, thus employed by a ſociety,
might overſee all the hives within two or three
counties in one ſeaſon; correcting, as he went a-
long, whatever he found amiſs either in the ſtate
or in the management of them, and ſtrictly en-
joining, that not a ſingle bee ſhould be killed at
any ſeaſon of the year. The increaſe of bee-
hives might alſo be rapidly forwarded, if proprietors of ground, upon giving leaſes to their
tenants, were to make it an article in their tack,
that the tenant ſhould furniſh the proprietor
with ſo many pints of honey produced upon

his

his own ground, annually, in proportion to the situation and extent of his farm, and for which he should be allowed the highest market price. And hints might be occasionally given in the newspapers, calling the attention of the public to perform the necessary offices about their bees, at the proper seasons of the year; as well as to inform the world when any new discovery of their nature, or improvement in their management, happens to be made.

Thus I have laid down a PLAN, in terms plain and intellegible to every capacity, for INCREASING THE NUMBER OF BEE-HIVES IN SCOTLAND; and have showed how HONEY and WAX may be increased to a PRODIGIOUS A-MOUNT, by a proper exertion upon the part of all who have any favourable situations for hives, but especially of gentlemen of property, who must be supposed to have the greatest variety of such advantages. And I now take farewell of my readers, by assuring them, upon the credit of near THIRTY YEARS EXPERIENCE, that the plan I have laid down is no chimæra, or *Will-o'-the-wisp*, but that, by strictly adhering to the preceding directions, they may depend upon meeting with the utmost success.

F I N I S.

INDEX.

INDEX,

A

ABORTIONS of bees, 128, 129, 130; *See* Bees, Eggs, and Hives.

Acre, one, of good land, will produce food for twenty hives, 12 ; one out of an hundred may be allotted for this purpose, 40.

Agency, free, bees endued with a high degree of, 127.

Agriculture, the Board of, the author's first meeting with the President, x. ; the happy consequences, *ib.* ; xi. ; the Board might encourage the culture of bees, 228.

Ale, mead a substitute for, 41 ; the face and hands should be be rubbed over with, previous to re-inforcing a hive, 130.

Ambassadors of the bees sometimes treated as spies, 188.

America, the author's plan will answer equally well for, as for Scotland, vi.

Ants, discovered sipping honey dew, 18 ; the fact confirmed by Boissier de Sauvages, 19: do little or no hurt to bees, 222 ; the contrary asserted by some, 223 ; how to guard against them, ib.

Apiary, the, directions respecting the situation of, 9, 10 ; a low one preferable, *ib.* ; free from wind and near plenty of flowers, *ib.* ; number of hives sufficient for one, 95 ; distance proper between each apiary, 96 ; necessary between the hives of different persons, 124 ; hives in the same apiary differ in number of inhabitants, 133 ; dead hives ought not to be allowed to remain in apiaries, 157, 158.

ib.; Reaumur's opinion, *ib.* 192; only carried into the hive while young bees are breeding, *ib.*

Bee-Burn, a rivulet in the parifh of Coldingham, 29,

Bee-Edge, a fteading in that parifh, 29.

Bee-Hives, See Hives.

Bee-mafter, fum proper to commence with, 5; fhould not be difcouraged by bad feafons, 9; fhould raife plenty of turnips, 12; and clover, 14; nothing fo adverfe to his intereft as the mutability of the weather, 29; ought to take care of his hives, 30; his feed time and harveft, 89; his refting time, 99; fhould pay particular attention to his hives in May, 131; need never be at a lofs for empty hives, 148; while fwarming, he fhould keep at a diftance till the bees fettle, 153.

Bee-Park, a fteading near Coldingham, 29.

Bees, the author appointed to watch his father's, iv; he contracts an early fondnefs for them, v; purchafes three hives, *ib.*; ftudies their nature, &c. *ib.*; (*see* Author,) pleafure and profit of keeping them, 1; contemplated by the ancients, *ib.*; and moderns, 2; the knowledge of them ftill in a ftate of infancy, *ib*; miftakes concerning them, *ib.*; encomium on their induftry, 3; fwarm twice in good years, 4; profits arifing from them, *ib.* 5, 6; rapid poffible increafe of them, *ib.*; poetical eulogium on them, 7; difcouraged by bad weather, *ib.*; the author refembles them, 8; their work retarded by wind, 9; though they fometimes thrive in fuch fituations, 10; pafturage proper for them, 11; bees very fond of the flowers of turnips, 12; rape, muftard, runches, 13; clover, 14; heath, furze, and broom, &c. 15; prefer fubftance to fhow, 16; continue to work on the fame kind of flowers they firft pitch on, *ib.*; extremely fond of honey dew, 18; make no change upon the honey, 20, 21; but only collect it, 22; working bees ought never to be killed, 24, 25; (*see* Killing;) bees formerly plentiful in Scotland, 28. 29; bad weather, the chief preventive of their thriving, 29; they will thrive, if they have but three days per week of good

G g weather,

Cafes

F

Famine, directions to preserve bees from, 110, 115, 131 ; *see* Food.

Farmers, gentlemen, advised to rear bees, 226, 227.

Feeding, see Combs, and Food.

Filth hurtful to bees, 223, 224.

Flowers, melifluous, the number of, in Britain almoft infinite, vi. ; the principal ones proper for bees, catalogue of, 11, 13, 14, 15 ; no kind of, refused by them, 16 ; thofe firft pitched on, preferred ever after, *ib.* ; honey contained in all flowers, 23 ; thoufands of millions of them in Scotland, 33, 34 ; artificial to be raifed, where natural ones fail, 40 ; various kinds recommended to be fown, 43, 44 : bees fly far in fearch of, 44, 45.

Food, directions how to fupply bees with, 110 ; four methods, 111, 113, 114, 115 ; weight of thofe hives that need fupplies, 125, 126 ; a hive with few bees will generally require none, 126 ; bees fhould be fed, when young drones are torn out before fwarming, 183 ; feeding combs fhould be placed before hives whofe fituations are changed, 187.

Frozen bees, method to recover, 106.

Furze, the flowers of, grateful to bees, 15 ; bloffoms early and continues long in flower, *ib.* ; advantage of rearing, 40 ; ought to be fown on dykes or wafte ground, 43.

G

Geddie, John, Efq; a writer on bees, 2 ; the inventor of colony hives, 147.

Generation of bees, a miftake concerning the, 2.

Gentleman, opinion of an intelligent, refpecting the change of fyrup into honey, 22, 23 ; his experiment in proof of this, 23 ; anecdote of another, 44.

Gentlemen of property, the increafe of Bee-hives begin to occupy the attention of, 26 ; called upon to exert themfelves,

27,

Highland

deſerted gradually, *ib.* ; ſtrong ones need no ſupply of food, 125 ; weight of thoſe that ſhould be ſupplied, *ib.*, 126 ; a thinly inhabited one requires none, 126 ; but a well-peopled one ought to be ſupplied, even though it ſhould not ſeem to need any, *ib.* ; a hive ruined when the Queen dies in ſpring, 127 ; ſigns that a hive is in this predicament, *ib.*, 128 ; and has been long without a Queen, 128 ; to diſtinguiſh abortive hives, 129 ; and how to manage them, 130 ; hives differ in the number of their inhabitants, 133 ; their entries ſhould be enlarged gradually in ſpring, 134; methods of doing this, *ib.* ; various circumſtances attending the ſwarming of hives, 150 ; previous ſymptoms, 151; hives whoſe bees are dead, preferred by young ſwarms, 156, 158 ; left ſtanding through knavery or ignorance, 157 ; criterion to diſtinguiſh between dead and living hives, 160 ; and when a hive will ſwarm a ſecond or third time, 162, 163 ; one large hive of more value than two ſmall ones, 167 ; weight and number of bees in hives, 168 ; how to treat a lying-out hive, 176, 178 ; a ſign of a thriving one, 180 ; advantages of changing the ſituation of hives to better paſture, 185, *et ſeq.* the removal ſhould be to a diſtance, 187 ; a numerous hive gradually decreaſes, 197, 198 ; but has often as much honey and wax as other four, *ib.* ; and ſtands a much better chance not to periſh, 199, 200 ; hives ſhould be always well ſtored with bees, 200 ; the bees of thoſe, from which honey is taken, ſhould be united to ſtock hives, *ib.* ; hives ſometimes become lighter after Auguſt, and ſometimes heavier, 201, *ſec* Habitation.

Honey-dealers of Scotland do not adulterate their honey, 215 ; only ſpoil it through ignorance, *ib.* ; are unjuſtly ſuſpected, *ib.*

Honey dew, diſquiſition concerning, 16 ; Mr Key's opinion of it, 17 ; found only on a few particular plants, *ib* ; and in fine weather, 18 ; the bees exceſſively fond of it, *ib.* ; ſipped by ants, *ib.* ; very ſeldom ſeen, 19 ; not once by the author upon oak leaves, *ib.* ; but on thoſe of runches and white thorn, *ib.*

Honey,

fifted in this work, 182; their manner of killing the drones, *ib.*; the author's manner, 183, 184; *see* Drones.

L.

Lammas, the fituations of bees fhould be changed about, 185.

Law, faid to be againſt allowing dead hives to ſtand in apiaries, 157; if not, it fhould be enacted, *ib.*; an erroneous decifion on this ſubject, *ib.*; would be a bad precedent, 158: no perfon would be fure of his ſwarms, *ib.*; difficulty ſtated, *ib.*, folved, *ib.*

Leafes, a hint refpecting the granting of, to tenants, 228.

Lime, plaſter, the ſkirts of hives fhould be clofed up with, and the entries ſtraitened, 96.

Loaded bees, time when they begin to appear, 132; at firſt can be eafily counted, 133; in the heat of fummer, defy all power of numeration, *ib.* *see* Bees, Hives, &c.

London, the author went from Berwick to, in order to converfe with Mr Wildman about bees, v; could carry an hundred bee-hives to, 140.

Lying-out hive, how to treat a, 176; *see* Hives, Swarming.

M.

Maggots, decayed, found in hives, 128; *see* Hives.

Man, hitherto the chief enemy of bees, 216, 217.

Management of bees, directions for the, in winter, 99, *et seq.* in March, April, and May, 121, *et seq.*, *see* Bees, Cold, Hives, &c.

March, bees begin to carry loads in, 125; directions how to manage bees in, 121, & *seq.* *see* Bees, Hives, &c.

Maxwell, R. a writer on bees, 2; quoted, 157.

May, how to manage bees in, 121, & *seq.* particular attention to be paid to bees this month, 131; how to choofe a hive at this period, 134; *see* Bees, Hives, Management, &c.

Mead, a fubftitute for ale and porter, 41; may be made

weak

weak or ftrong from the honey that remains in the combs, 207, 208.

Meliſſus, king of Crete, the inventor of bee-hives, 144; would probably never have been heard of otherwife, 228.

Melody of the humming of bees, a remedy for chagrin, 227.

Mice, the moſt pernicious enemies to bees, 97, 217; deſtroy hundreds of hives annually, 97.

Millions, the only proper numerator for the flowers of Scotland, 33, 34; *see* Flowers, Hives, Honey, Increaſe, &c.

Miſtakes concerning bees, 2, 53, 68, 70, 73, 104; ſpecimen of, 2; corrected, 44, 45, 53, 54, 73, 104, 199, 213.

Moorland fituations, turnips and rape, proper for, 13.

Mother bee, the proper name of the Queen bee, 52; her age when ſhe becomes a mother, 200; *see* Queen

Murderers of bees, man, one of the chief, 216, 217, *see* Killing.

Muſic of bees, invites different ſwarms to join each other, 166, 167; a remedy for chagrin or melancholy, 227.

Muſtard, one of the principal plants from which bees extract honey, 11; they are very fond of its flowers, 13; ſhould be ſown at different periods, to protract the flowering ſeaſon, *ib.* 14, 43.

N.

National importance, honey and wax objects of, 27, 40, 41.

Neceſſaries, honey might be made a ſubſtitute for ſome, 41.

Neighbouring proprietors of bees ſhould join in providing flowers, 46.

Newcaſtle, the ladies and gentlemen of, fond of the honey produced from heath, 214.

News-papers, hints, reſpecting the management of bees, might occaſionally be given in, 228, 229

Noiſe, improper when a ſwarm are riſing, 152; but neceſſary when they attempt to fly off, *ib.*; in general hurtful to bees, 223; how to guard againſt it, *ib.*

O.

O.

Oak, the leaves of, honey dew found on, 18, 19.

Oeconomy rural, the culture of bees a branch of, within the reach of the poorest cottager, vii.

Old people, the increase of bee hives would afford employ-ment for, 48, 49, 150.

Order and regularity great among bees, 53.

Over-stocking fields with bees, no danger of, 34, 35, 36.

Oziers, the flowers of, afford honey and work for bees, 15.

P.

Parnaſſus, account of a repaſt of honey at, 225.

Pariſhes, ſome, that have not twenty hives, might maintain three hundred, 32 ; a thouſand hives in each would not extract the half of the honey in their flowers, 37.

Parliament, an act of, ſhould be paſſed, if no law already ex-iſts, againſt allowing dead hives to remain in apiaries, 157.

Paſturage of bees, ii. *ſee* Flowers, Muſtard, Rape, &c.

Paſture, good, bees thrive beſt near, 10.

Patriots called upon to attend to the ſubject of this treatiſe, 27.

Paucity of bee-hives, reaſons for the, in Scotland, 28, 29, 30.

Philiſcus, a contemplator of bees, 2.

Philoſophers puzzled to account for the diverſity of talents among mankind, iii. ; antient, who contemplated bees, 1. 2, 144 ; bees worthy the attention of, 3 ; colony hives uſe-ful to the inquiſitive, 147.

Plane-trees, the flowers of, afford food for bees, 13 ; highly agreeable to them, *ib.* ; ought to be planted on purpoſe, 43.

Pleaſure of keeping bees, 1, 3 ; of the bee-maſter in ſeeing his hives ſwarming, 151, 152 ; *ſee* Bees, Hives, &c.

Poetical eulogium on bees, 7 ; picture of their wars, 117.

Poland, a market for purchaſing bees cheap, 49.

Poor among mankind, bees reſemble the, 16 ; the culture of bees would afford employment for, 48, 49.

Poor bee-masters advised to raise turnips, 12 ; in general make more of their bees than the rich, 30 ; the reason why, 31 ; bees, a sort of estate to them, *ib.* ; advised to sell their hives, 47.

Porter, mead a substitute for, 41.

Poverty of many bee-masters, a cause of the paucity of bee-hives, 31.

Powers, prolific, of the Queen, amazing, 198, 199 ; depend much on the state of the hive, 199 ; of the cod fish, *ib.*

Practicability of increasing the number of bee-hives, ix. *see* hives.

Preface, iii. *et seq.*

Premiums, small, might be given to encourage the culture of bees, 228,

Prices received and paid for honey and wax, 38, 39 ; would be reduced by the proposed increase of bee-hives, 41. 42.

Princesses, young Queens, their proclamations, 163. *see* Queen.

Profit of keeping bees, 4, 5, 6, 38, 39.

O.

Queen bee, a mistake concerning the, 2 ; described, 50, 51 ; very pacific, 51 ; ought to be called the mother bee, as she lays all the eggs, 52 ; and exerts no sovereignty, *ib.* ; is anxious for the good of the commonwealth, *ib.* ; errors respecting her, 53 ; refuted, *ib.* 54 ; can be raised from a common egg, *ib* ; can lay eggs to produce bees, and become a mother without seeing a drone, 55 ; experiment in proof of this, *ib.* 56 ; distress of the bees for want of their Queen, 57 ; they raise another, *ib.* ; who lays eggs, 58 ; another experiment, *ib.* ; objections, *ib.* 59 ; answered, 59 ; method of rearing a Queen, 60 ; gradual metamorphosis, 61 ; doubtful whether every egg in a common cell can be raised to be a Queen, 62 ; the author has caused two hundred artificial Queens to be reared, 63 ; sign when a Queen may be depended upon, 64 ; difficulties respecting the matter injected into the royal cells, 65 ; more Queen bees raised than are needed for swarms, 66 ; the

supernumerary

Rape

Sauvages,

tween

Virgil

fronted, they feldom ufe their ftings, 82 ; extremely irritable, *ib.* ; directions how to handle them, *ib.* ; their organs
of fmelling very acute, 84 ; they never fting when at work,
85 ; (*see* fting ;) not one of them fhould be killed, 200.

Worms, filk, analogous to bees, 196.

Y

Years peculiarly favourable to bees, viii. 4, 9, 105 ; probable
increafe of hives in ten, 5 ; ditto in feven, 47, 48 ; years
hurtful to bees, 104.

Yellow, the fields and bees legs equally fo, in May, 133.

Young bees fometimes found decayed in the cells, 128 ; (*see*
Bees and Cells ;) the more will be hatched, the longer the
old ones remain in the hives, 202 ; how to preferve the
young brood, when the honey is taken, *ib.*, 203.

Young fwarms fometimes defert their hives, 123, *see* fwarming.

Z

Zeal, patriotic, of the bees, in defence of their Queen and hive,
170, 171, *see* Queen, Wars, &c.

ADVERTISEMENT.

Any Gentleman, or Lady, who may be defirous of confulting or employing the Author of this work, with regard to the Management of Bees, in any refpect, upon addreffing a line to him at Mr GRANT'S, *Leith Wynd, Edinburgh, will be duely waited upon.*

The Author embraces this opportunity of returning his beft thanks to his numerous cuftomers in general, and to thofe of this metropolis in particular, for the very liberal encouragement he has repeatedly met with from them as a Honey Dealer; and begs that they will favour him with their orders, as early as poffible, for the honey of the enfuing feafon, to prevent danger of being difappointed.

EDINBURGH,   }
July 18. 1795. }

ERRATA.

Page v Line 19th, For *both* read *all three.*
— 9 — 7th, For *does* read *do.*
— 21 — 21st, For *conniosseurs* read *connoisseurs.*
— 22 — 18th, For *meant* read *meat.*
— 22 — 27th, For *gentlemen* read *gentleman.*
— 27 — 26th, For *an article* read *articles.*
— 29 — 4th, For *preventative* read *preventive.*
— 31 — 21st, and 22d, For *she prove a bad one and die,* read *most or all of the bees die.*
— 37 — 16th, For 80,000, read 320,000.
— 47 — 29th, For *counties* read *countries.*
— 76 — 7th, For *breed* read *bred.*
— 120 — 19th, For *some sore* read *a bloody.*
— 136 — 17th, For *her* read *it.*
— 149 — 2d, For *lon* read *lion.*
— — — 12th, For XIX read XX.
— 158 — 2d, For *no* read *every.*
— 159 — 13th, For *as* read *that.*
— — — 21st, For *brush* read *bush.*
— 199 — 8th, For SWAMMERDANE read SWAMMERDAM.
— 210 — 3d, For *lever* read *sleeve.*
— 215 — 2d, For *flower,* read *flour.*
— — — 19th, For *fomented* read *fermented.*